# The Thames
# at War

Blitz on the River, September 1940. (*Mary Evans Picture Library:* © *London Fire Brigade 10534574*)

# The Thames
# at War

### Gustav Milne
### &
### The Thames Discovery Programme

PEN & SWORD
HISTORY

First published in Great Britain in 2020 by
**PEN & SWORD HISTORY**
An imprint of
Pen & Sword Books Ltd
47 Church Street
Barnsley
South Yorkshire
S70 2AS

ISBN 978-1-52676-802-5

Typeset by Concept, Huddersfield HD4 5JL.
Printed and bound in England by TJ International Ltd, Padstow, Cornwall.

Pen & Sword Books Limited incorporates the imprints of Atlas, Archaeology, Aviation, Discovery, Family History, Fiction, History, Maritime, Military, Military Classics, Politics, Select, Transport, True Crime, Air World, Frontline Publishing, Leo Cooper, Remember When, Seaforth Publishing, The Praetorian Press, Wharncliffe Local History, Wharncliffe Transport, Wharncliffe True Crime and White Owl.

For a complete list of Pen & Sword titles please contact
PEN & SWORD BOOKS LIMITED
47 Church Street, Barnsley, South Yorkshire, S70 2AS, England
E-mail: enquiries@pen-and-sword.co.uk
Website: www.pen-and-sword.co.uk

# Contents

# Introduction

The Thames was once the lifeblood of London. It brought traffic, trade and prosperity to the city and, as its industries and wealth grew, so too did its population. Yet that close dependency on the river also had disadvantages. It could flood when the tidal cycle and the weather combined malevolently, as happened in 1928 and 1953 with disastrous consequences. Then again, during the Blitz, the very familiar sinuous shape of the Thames directed waves of bombers to valuable targets. Even at night, regardless of an enforced black-out, the river could be dramatically illuminated by moonlight leading the Luftwaffe straight to warehouses, industries, power stations, offices, docks and the associated housing.

It was that image of London's river blindly facilitating its own destruction that lead to the development of the Thames at War project. This was organized by the Thames Discovery Programme (TDP), the community-based team focused particularly on recording foreshore archaeology, those sites and features only exposed when the tide is out. During our surveys, examples of battered and rebuilt river walls were noticed: could some be surviving evidence of bomb damage to our river defences in the Blitz? Was this seen as a serious problem in the 1940s? Had the extent of this waterfront destruction been recorded and, if so, where? As a result of ten years' foreshore fieldwork and research in the London Metropolitan Archives, a sobering story was uncovered that answered those questions.

\*　\*　\*

From 1940 to 1945 the German Air Force (the Luftwaffe) inflicted 101 day-light and 253 night-time air-raids on London. The Blitz caused more than 80,000 fatalities or serious injuries and extensive devastation. In all that may-hem caused by high explosives, incendiaries, parachute mines, rockets and firestorms, the city was also faced with another threat. This was the very real possibility of major flooding whenever bombing seriously breached the river wall. This report tells the hitherto unappreciated story of how the London County Council's (LCC's) emergency repair teams rose to that particular challenge and saved London from drowning. The study was conducted by the Thames Discovery Programme, the community-based archaeological team engaged in fieldwork on the foreshore and research in the London Metropolitan Archives.

Part One presents the background to the work of the LCC's Thames-Flood Prevention Emergency Repairs team (known as 'T-F', 'Thames-Flood'), and an overview of their activities during the Blitz.

Part Two provides a catalogue of incidents dealt with by each of the four regional T-F depots, located on the Isle of Dogs, in Southwark, Battersea and Greenwich, together with the work in the City of London itself.

Part Three considers the role of the other rapid-response units operating on the Thames during this period, particularly the Auxiliary Fire Service (AFS, later the National Fire Service) who would have often worked alongside T-F teams. This is followed by a description of the LCC's work on the bridges that crossed the Thames and the damage inflicted on them during the Blitz, concluding with an assessment of the important work undertaken by the T-F service.

Part Four widens the perspective with a summary study of ships, boats and barges wrecked on the Thames during the Second World War, incorporating further archaeological survey work and research by the Thames Discovery Programme team.

Throughout this book, the term 'Blitz' describes not just the intensive aerial bombardment of September 1940 to May 1941 (often referred to as the 'London Blitz') but also the subsequent attacks by bombers and rockets up to March 1945.

Gustav Milne

Museum of London Archaeology, 46 Eagle Wharf Road, London N1 7ED

UCL Institute of Archaeology, 31–34 Gordon Square, London WC1H 0PY

# Acknowledgements

This study is the work of the TDP team, which was formally established in 2008, with a generous grant from the Heritage Lottery Fund. Based initially at University College London, it is now hosted by Museum of London Archaeology (MOLA). Its hardworking officers – particularly Nathalie Cohen and Eliott Wragg – supported the project from the outset, while Helen Johnston, Josh Frost and Will Rathouse ably assisted subsequently.

An army of dedicated Foreshore Research and Observation Group members then visited, recorded and researched the many sites discussed in this book. First and foremost is Peter Kennedy who set the ball rolling, as is confirmed by the many photographs he took which now appear in this publication. Others took up the challenge, including Jonathan Aldridge, Lynn Baldwin, Carol Bentley, Angela Broomfield, Hannah Bullmore, Glen Calderwood, Chris Chadwick, Amber Cottee, Susan Cottee, Niall Counihan, Gillian Crossan, Hilary Davies, Maureen Dennis, Jan Drew, Hugh Dulley, Vanita Eden, Nicola Fyfe, Jenny Fisher, Alice Gibbs, Chris Gunstone, Michael Hargrave, Keith Harmon, Alan Harris, Martin Hatton, Greer Hill, Mick Hodges, Arwen James, Helen Johnston, Paw Jorgenson, Meg Latham, John Layt, Daphne Keen, Adam and Robert Kerry, Jeanne Lewis, John Lingford, Ken Marks, Yvonne Masson, Kate Masters, Paula Melville, Claire Millington, Graeme Mitchell, Jeff Pywell, John Richardson, Nic Shore, Jennifer Simonson, Margaret Sparks, Selina Springbett, Brian Stanley, Sarah Stanley, Graham Strudwick, Ann Sydney, Guy Taylor, Suzanne Taylor, Roland Petchey, Sophie Radicke, Tom Robinson, Solange la Rose, Sue Rowell, Pat Wakeham, Josephine Warren, Marion Watson, Shamayim Watson, Luke Whitelaw, Jean Whiting, Tim Wilkins and Edna Wolfson.

The debt to the authors of the works listed in the Bibliography is also warmly and fully acknowledged, as are the comments, advice and information that were generously offered by Major Edwin Hunt, Andy Brockman, Chris Ellmers, the Frank family, Bill Hickin, Rachel Hill, Therese Kearns, Chris Kolonko, Sally Mashiter, the Medway Queen Preservation Trust, Eric Rawlinson, Jane Sidell, Victor Smith and Edwin Trout.

Then there are the staff at publishers Pen & Sword, the London Metropolitan Archives, the Museum of London Picture Gallery, the Mary Evans collection, many colleagues at Museum of London Archaeology, including

Thames Discovery Programme (TDP): a team photo on the Westminster foreshore, having just recorded evidence of a major bomb strike there some eighty years earlier. (© *TDP, N. Cohen*)

Tracy Wellman, Mark Burch and Catherine Drew, and at University College London, such as Charlotte Frearson and Sue Harrington.

The researchers would like to state their appreciation of the photographers of London in the 1930s and 1940s, many of whose evocative images appear in this book; the perceptive George Reid; the PLA and Fire Brigade teams; and the remarkable Arthur Cross and Frank Tibbs, whose images of the Blitz as it happened are seared into the collective memory.

We are happy to acknowledge that grants towards the costs of publication of this book were most gratefully received from the MARC FITCH FUND.

## MARC FITCH FUND

# Abbreviations

| | |
|---|---|
| AA | Anti-Aircraft |
| AFS | Auxiliary Fire Service |
| ARP | Air-Raid Precautions |
| CE | Chief Engineer (Sir Thomas Peirson Frank held this post for LCC from 1930 to 1946) |
| HE | High-explosive (as opposed to incendiary) |
| IWT | Internal Water Transport |
| LCC | London County Council |
| LMA | London Metropolitan Archives |
| MOL | Museum of London |
| MOLA | Museum of London Archaeology |
| NFS | National Fire Service |
| OD | Ordnance Datum: notional figure representing a mathematical mean sea level |
| RE | Royal Engineers |
| TDP | Thames Discovery Programme |
| T-F | 'Thames-Flood', abbreviation for LCC's Thames-Flood Prevention Emergency Repairs team |
| V-1 | German 'Vengeance Weapon 1', Pilotless Air Craft also known as doodlebug or flying Bomb |
| V-2 | German 'Vengeance Weapon 2', supersonic rocket |

# PART ONE

# A SECRET HISTORY

# Chapter One

# An Untold Story

We have all heard of the famous 'Dam Busters' attack in 1943, when the RAF's 617 Squadron breached two dams in the Ruhr valley, Germany's industrial heartland. The subsequent flood from that single raid devastated a vast area, seriously damaged many armaments factories vital to the Nazi war effort, and drowned more than 1,000 souls. However, London is also low-lying and thus very vulnerable to flooding: what if the Luftwaffe had breached our river walls during the Blitz and inundated our own conurbation? What if they could flood basements of buildings and the underground system, where so many Londoners sought refuge from the bombing? We all know that our flood defences were not compromised during the dark days of the Blitz, but it is not widely appreciated how close we came to such a catastrophe. Unpublished records in the London Metropolitan Archives reveal the bad news: the river wall was hit more than 100 times between 1940 and 1945.The good news is that not one of these potentially serious breaches resulted in a major flood. This raises a couple of questions:

How did London survive the Blitz without being flooded?
Why has this story remained untold for so long?

The answer to the first question lies with the London County Council's rapid-response unit, called the Thames-Flood Prevention Emergency Repairs service or Thames-Flood (T-F) for short. This book summarizes its work, based on a study of the LCC's Chief Engineer's correspondence files – the gentleman in question was one Thomas Peirson Frank – and the two original hand-written log books compiled by the T-F team. These records are now lodged in the London Metropolitan Archives, but do not seem to have been studied in any detail for seventy years.

The answer to the second question is surprising simple: the work of the T-F unit was conducted without publicity and, like so much else during the war, information on it was suppressed. Even during peacetime, the British press could be muzzled; the only Britons who were aware of the impending abdication crisis in 1936, for example, were those who could access American newspapers. In wartime censorship was even more rigorous. It is now known, for example, that the publication of bomb damage to particular buildings was deliberately delayed for up to twenty-eight days so that the Luftwaffe would

Germany calling: a Heinkel 111 bomber, intent on destruction, flies over the West India, Millwall and Surrey Docks on 7 September 1940. The Luftwaffe targeted the Thames, its warehouses, waterfront industries, factories, docks, housing and shipping, but did it also try to breach London's flood defences? (*Mary Evans Picture Library: © Everett Collection 11001639*)

be less able to assess the effectiveness of particular bombing raids. In the interest of public morale, not one photograph of any of 18,688 civilian fatalities from the Blitz was ever passed for publication, while information on the V-1 and V-2 attacks was carefully censored until the nature of the rockets was better understood. Indeed, the major and extensive preparations for the evacuation of a quarter of a million Londoners in 1945 – a response to the assault by those rockets – was also not discussed openly.

Similar reasoning lies behind the secrecy that shrouded Thames-Flood: on the one hand it was thought that Londoners' morale had quite enough to cope with while dealing with fire and high explosives without accentuating the very real threat of flooding. In addition, any public reporting of flood damage might only serve to alert the Luftwaffe to the real vulnerability of beleaguered London. So the work of the Thames-Flood team continued throughout the war, as unknown to the vast majority of Londoners (even those who lived and worked close to the main depots) as it was to the Luftwaffe.

An unpublished personal account by Mick Pitt underlines this point. He records a significant incident at Teddington Lock, the facility that artificially maintained the river's tidal head. In 1941, an explosion and a pall of smoke over the lock attracted him to the Thames, where hundreds of dead and stunned fish were being hurriedly harvested after a stick of bombs had exploded in the river. Unfortunately, one bomb had hit the weir island, destroying it and the sluice gates that controlled the river's flow. By the next day, the river there had all but dried up, now being confined to a narrow channel on its wide bed, and it took weeks before the sluices were rebuilt. During this period, the river was no longer navigable beyond this point, just at a time when petrol rationing had turned the Thames into a major highway. Barges carrying coal and materials could not get up to Oxford, and Vosper's boatyards upriver at Walton, where they built motor torpedo boats, could not dispatch their craft to the Royal Navy. As Mick Pitts wryly commented in a BBC interview in July 2005: 'Not a word of the Thames's humiliation ever appeared in the newspapers. Wartime security, denying the enemy the satisfaction of publicity, saw to that.' The remains of the original bomb-damaged

Bombing the river: the artificial tidal head of the Thames is here at Teddington, where a weir controls the river's flow. This photo shows the battered timber remains of an earlier weir in the foreground with the modern rebuilt structure behind. (© *TDP, L. Baldwin*)

Shock and awe: the Blitz began on 7 September 1940 with a ferocious attack on the London docks. (*Mary Evans Picture Library:* © *Everett Collection 11000751*)

weir can still be seen at Teddington, and have been recorded by Lynn Baldwin of the Thames Discovery Programme. However, taking such photographs in 1941 would have been a questionable activity back then.

Hilary Davies records that her mother was aged 19 in 1940 when the London Blitz began with a vengeance on 7 September. By chance she was staying with a friend, whose father was a caretaker in the City. He had a rooftop flat there, from which the girls could see the whole of the Surrey Docks ablaze. Oblivious of the danger to themselves, they stood there hypnotized as the apocalypse unfolded in front of them, breathing in the smoke from burning leather, tea and sugar. She then subsequently served as an air-raid warden, an ambulance driver and in the Women's Home Guard. That pattern of initial disbelief followed by resolute, robust action is how much of London's civilian population responded, and such robust action was demanded not just by all the civilian-staffed emergency services but by the Thames-Flood rapid-response teams too.

We know more about the Thames-Flood unit today than most Londoners ever did in 1940. Thanks to Peter Kennedy, a detailed study has now been made of the LCC's hand-written Incident Log Books, as well as letters and sundry correspondence relating to the setting-up of the depots, staffing and costs, all now carefully curated in the London Metropolitan Archives. From these primary data it proved possible to build up a picture of how the organization was established and how it went about its day-to-day (or night-to-night) business. We also have a handful of original incident report forms, made within hours, or perhaps minutes, of a bomb strike. The log books themselves were written up slightly later, perhaps on a weekly basis, bringing

Citizen Science: the Thames Discovery Programme's research project rediscovered log books used by LCC's Thames-Flood Prevention Emergency Repair team in 1940–45. Although catalogued in the London Metropolitan Archives, they had remained unopened for seventy years. (© *LMA: TDP, P. Kennedy*)

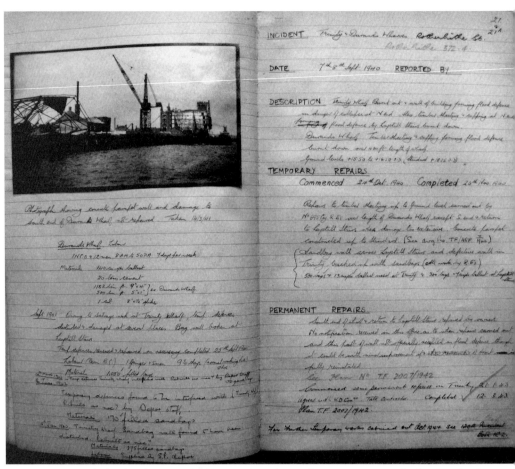

War record: this hand-written double-page spread provides a succinct record of an 'incident', giving the date of the bomb strike, brief damage description, how it was repaired and how long that process took. (© *LMA: TDP, P. Kennedy*)

together reports from all four of the T-F operational depots. The numbering system used to list the 'incidents' is broadly chronological, but the sequence is occasionally thrown by a delay in reporting or in a decision to renumber a site (e.g. 13 and 13a), or where a site suffered a later second hit. A fresh page is allocated to each 'incident', and a later hand then notes when the 'temporary repairs' were started/completed, and then when the 'permanent repairs' were started/completed. Clearly the officers were concerned not just with first-aid but with the longer-term health of the patient.

## An Archaeology of a River's War

To the study of that primary documentary evidence, an archaeological dimension has now been added. Since the fiftieth anniversary of the end of the Second World War in the 1990s, there has been an increasing interest in the study of that all-consuming conflict and now it has become an acceptable subject, not just for military or social historians but also for archaeological research. The Defence of Britain project, which was initiated by the Council for British Archaeology in 1996, was one of the first major projects that looked systematically at sites from the 1940s, while the 2013 study of Britain's wartime heritage by Gabriel Moshenka shows how diverse such investigations can be. One such project was run by the Thames Discovery Programme, a community archaeology project based at University College London and at the Museum of London. It involved us in the survey of archaeological sites of many different dates that are exposed on the foreshore at low tide. During 2009–10, attention to the river walls enabled the recording of examples of 1940s' repair work that were still visible. This exercise was as exhilarating as it was sobering; we can now report that London still has some remarkable monuments to the Blitz incorporated into its modern flood defences.

However, first we had to find the potential sites; not always an easy task. The strikes to the river wall were not consistently shown on the LCC's 'Bomb-Damage Maps 1939–45', as this haunting survey was drawn up to show the scale of the damage to the built fabric of London, the buildings for which the LCC had a measure of responsibility. Strikes to Buckingham Palace or the Houses of Parliament are not shown, neither are craters in the road nor the breaches in the flood defences or to tunnels under the Thames. Many of the names by which the Thames-Flood sites were known in 1940 have also long since disappeared, even Pyrimont Wharf, the site of the busiest

The Thames Discovery Programme at work: community archaeology on the Millwall foreshore in 2010. (© *TDP, N. Cohen*)

of the T-F's depots, is today unmarked and unknown on the Isle of Dogs. So many of the names and locations of wharves and former factories have gone as the Blitz subsequently changed London's nomenclature as much as its topography.

For a substantial reach of the pre-war river, however, help was at hand in the form of the superb 'London's Lost Riverscape' photographic survey from 1937, i.e. just before so much was swept away. Working with this admirable study published in 1988, with its copious and informative notes by Chris Ellmers and Alex Werner, many an otherwise unlocated name was duly and rapidly rediscovered, at least for the sites to the east of the City. For the rest of the river, the scrutiny of early maps and local historical studies provided most of the answers. Once the 'incident location' was duly plotted onto one of today's maps, then the adjacent foreshore was visited. The ground-truthing programme was successfully instigated by Peter Kennedy and extended by other TDP members. Although a cliff of modern sheet piling was often found obscuring the site of the T-F team's efforts, it nevertheless proved possible to find sufficient examples of 1940s' river wall repair work to make the survey more than worthwhile.

Blast damage: the TDP team recording debris scatter from a river wall bomb strike at Westminster. (© *TDP, N. Cohen*)

Nautical archaeology on the foreshore: the TDP team at Tripcock Ness, 2012. (© *TDP, N. Cohen*)

## In Perspective

There have been many books written on the Blitz, as the bibliography in Ziegler's 2002 study shows. These include the *Official History* published by HMSO in 1942, packed with the now famous black-and-white images that most certainly shaped at least one incredulous schoolboy's understanding of that period. The role of the Auxiliary Fire Service and later the National Fire Service should never be underestimated, as the studies by Eric Jackson and Bill Hickin show. It is also commemorated in the remarkable film *Fires Were Started* directed by Humphrey Jennings, using serving NFS personnel based at 36B1 auxiliary station in Wellclose Square, Stepney and at the warehouses in Pennington Street. There are reports on military matters, such as the anti-aircraft batteries and Maunsell Forts that defended the estuary from airborne attacks (these coastal defences were not decommissioned until the 1950s). Then there were the booms off Shoeburyness and off St Mary's Bay, and the armed tugs and launches of the Thames Auxiliary Naval Force to protect against enemy seaborne incursions and parachute mines. Finally, there was the network of riverside pillboxes and other entrenchments and obstacles to

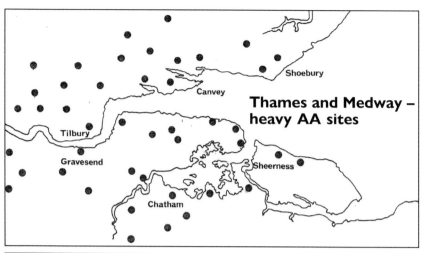

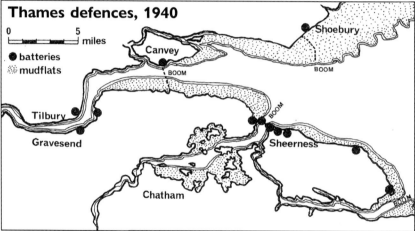

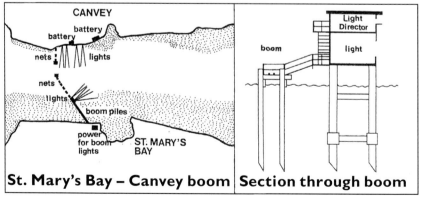

Defending our river: the disposition of anti-submarine and anti-aircraft defences in the outer Thames Estuary in the 1940s. (*By kind permission of V.T.C. Smith*)

delay or constrain any possible invasion force. The latter were not tested after the Battle of Britain forced Hitler to abort his attempted invasion of England, but all the other organizations saw more than enough action (Dobinson 2001, Smith 1985, pp. 41–8).

Social perspectives are provided by local histories such as Eve Hosteller's compilation of life on the Isle of Dogs and by wider studies, including that by Juliet Gardiner. The grievous architectural losses have also been evaluated in studies dating from 1941 to 1980, while the extraordinary work undertaken by the staff of London Transport to keep the network going and to repair the horrendous damage to their infrastructure is, to say the least, illuminating.

The understated heroism of such non-combatants is also evident in several studies on the war on the river. One of the best overviews is *The Thames on Fire*, published in 1985 by Lieutenant Commander L.M. Bates, who summarizes the action from so many waterfront vantage points as London's riverside communities kept calm and tried to carry on. To take just one example from his absorbing book, he recounts the crucial role played by the Thames simply maintaining gas and electricity supplies in a town the size of London: Blitz or no Blitz, some 13 million tons of coal had to be delivered each year to the power stations on the riverbank, all by fleets of colliers. These modest merchant vessels sailing down the east coast from Newcastle now faced mines in the North Sea and Thames Estuary, bombing and strafing from the Luftwaffe, and torpedoes from U-boats and E-boats. During the course of the war, the Gas Light and Coke Co. lost nine vessels, the South Metropolitan Gas Co. four out of its fleet of seven, and Stephenson Clarke Ltd lost four in one week, while the Wandsworth & District Gas Co. only lost half a collier (the stern was salvaged). The colliers working for the Borough of Fulham's Electricity Dept had many lucky escapes; they even opened fire on enemy aircraft and brought down at least one. Somehow, the 'black gold' got through.

On the wider stage, London's 'Little Ships' served in Operation DYNAMO at Dunkirk in 1940. London's docks were later used to build sections of the great Mulberry Harbours for Operation OVERLORD, as well as the conversion of some 1,200 Thames barges and lighters to provide the essential logistical support for the Allied forces on the Normandy beaches for the D-Day landings in 1944. It was London's lightermen and stevedores that served on those craft, ensuring that essential munitions, tanks and even cooked meals were delivered to the troops as they fought their way up the beach, through France and into the Low Countries (Edwin Hunt, pers. comm.). The River Thames Formation, part of the National Fire Service, also played a role in the invasion since two flotillas were initially established to form the Overseas Fireboat Contingent.

Made in London: the last prefabricated Mulberry Harbour unit in George V Dock, ready to be towed across the Channel to Normandy in June 1944. (© *Museum of London PLA Collection 33933*)

The contribution that London's river made to the war effort was therefore rather more than 'just' passive resistance: 'London can take it' was a familiar phrase, but many non-combatant civilians showed extraordinary resolute courage on a daily basis. All the works cited here show that, as do the detailed studies of particular themes, such as the Port of London Authority's war, studies of the damage to the docks and to the dockland communities.

All that said, not one of these books or reports makes mention of the Thames-Flood service. The summary published here hopes to make good that omission, setting one of the LCC's secret contributions to the war effort alongside all those other civilian teams who fought the good fight.

*Chapter Two*

# A Metropolis Susceptible to Flooding: 1928–39

### Lessons to be Learned

Low-lying London depended on the Thames for its livelihood, but that great transport artery was not always beneficent as it burst its banks whenever a conjunction of high tides, storm surges or poor waterfront maintenance allowed. Such catastrophes are recorded as far back as the medieval and Tudor periods. In more recent times, dangerously high tides occurred with an almost inevitable regularity and an alarming upward increase in height in 1791, 1834,

Submerged city: the capital was totally unprepared for the severe flood of 1928; a hard lesson from which London needed to learn. Official emergency services were slow to respond: this image from low-lying Bermondsey in south-east London shows how local communities were left to fend for themselves. (© *Mary Evans Picture Library 10698673*)

Flood tide: the unexpected height reached by the high tide in January 1928 is marked by plaques, such as this one near the Albert Bridge. (© *TDP, A. Broomfield*)

1852, 1874 and 1881. It was a mathematical certainty that worse was to come. On the night of 7 January 1928, the heart of the Imperial capital of the British Empire awoke to find itself under water. The highest spring tide since 1881 had overtopped the river walls in Bermondsey, in Southwark, the Embankment at Westminster, and further upstream at Putney and Hammersmith. The moat at the Tower of London was flooded, the basement of the Tate Gallery was under water and Lambeth Bridge was undermined. Worst of all, part of the adjacent river wall collapsed, causing a flood that damaged hundreds of buildings and drowned people sleeping in basements. Such catastrophes were not supposed to happen in Central London. Questions were asked, especially of London County Council, the authority that included flood prevention among its many responsibilities. Its Chief Engineer retired

In 1928 flood waters inundated acres of land on both banks of the river across the capital. Note the plaque on the river wall to left of the steps. (© *TDP, A. Broomfield*)

shortly afterwards, and a new man was brought in to ensure that such disasters would never happen again.

## Thomas Peirson Frank

London's next Chief Engineer was born in Yorkshire in 1881 and began his career in the sewers of Dewsbury and then in Ripon with work on two river dams before moving to Stockton-on-Tees. His life as a borough engineer was interrupted by the Great War when he was posted to France in 1915 with the Royal Engineers. Although wounded in action, he continued his military service as a lecturer at the School of Instruction before being demobilized in 1918 with the rank of captain. Moving on to Plymouth as borough engineer, he designed major reinforced concrete landing stages, roads and sewers. Clearly an ambitious man, he went on to hold posts at the leading ports of Cardiff and Liverpool, at which he was responsible for a major waterfront development at Southport, for example.

Finally, in 1930, he was appointed to the post of Chief Engineer for London County Council, the most prestigious such post in the land. The work here

Cometh the hour, cometh the man: Portrait by Frank Salisbury of Sir Thomas Peirson Frank 1891–1951, Chief Engineer for London County Council during the dark days of the Blitz. (© *The Estate of Frank O. Salisbury*)

involved many issues such as improving main drainage, housing estates and sewage installations, but a key item on the agenda was, unsurprisingly, refurbishing the river defences. His department also oversaw the completion of Lambeth Bridge, the widening of Putney Bridge, the building of Wandsworth Bridge and Chelsea Bridge, and the demolition and rebuilding of Waterloo Bridge. He thus became very familiar with the Thames and the riverside boroughs. In addition to his work with LCC he also maintained his military connections, becoming a colonel in the Engineer and Railway Staff Corps, serving as an instructor from 1932 onwards. It is worth recalling that he also served on several government committees, advising on 'Health in Garden Cities and Satellite Towns' (1932–34), the Highways Research Board (1935–40) and the National Consultative Council of the Building and Civil Engineering Industries (1942–44). He was planning for the future while dealing with the present.

As the threat of another war increased in the 1930s, that future was, to say the least, uncertain. The last war had seen London suffering from air-raids, with bombs delivered by aeroplanes as well as Zeppelins. Technology had advanced over the last twenty years, and a town the size of London, set as it was on the banks of such a readily-identifiable river, offered an easy target from the air, by day or by night. This was a threat to be taken seriously and, behind the scenes, serious preparations were duly made, though not always by a government still, perhaps understandably, hoping for peace. For example, realists in the Cement and Concrete Association, well aware of the civilian bombings during the Spanish Civil War, made no excuses for their public intervention in preparations for the looming war in Britain with their robust advocacy of concrete-built air-raid shelters, as Edwin Trout's research shows. Although partially driven by commercial self-interest, this ensured that the country was far better prepared for the Blitz than it might have been and, by 1939, the cement industry selflessly put all its resources at the disposal of the government for the duration. They were much needed, and concrete became a key resource for the protection of Londoners; it was also commonly used for the permanent repairs of its breached river defences.

To take another example, several of the London Underground lines ran under the Thames, and if the roof of any one of eleven tunnels was destroyed, then much of the subterranean network would be flooded, as would the stations themselves and the escalator chambers. The remedy was to install massive floodgates, watertight doors and tunnel diaphragms: this major work programme cost £1m and installation commenced in September 1938. This was the same month in which Prime Minister Neville Chamberlain returned from negotiations in Germany with a letter signed by Herr Hitler, allegedly securing peace in our time. The London Transport Passenger Board, like Winston Churchill, was unconvinced and was leaving nothing to chance.

However, it was not just the Underground that was at risk. Should London's river walls be breached during an intense aerial bombardment, then the sprawling city could all too easily add the scourge of flooding to devastation from fire and high explosives. The floodable area of London contained a population of more than 1 million with 300,000 dwellings, most of the port's offices and warehouses (with their stored foodstuffs and manufactured goods), and several major power stations. The majority of the telephone network was powered by underground accumulators, all of which could be put out of action; the gas, electricity and drinking water supplies would be at risk; while the back-flow from drains and sewers would provide further problems. As for the potential human cost, with Londoners sheltering in basements, Tube stations and other underground facilities, it was soon appreciated by those that did the sums how grave the situation could be. All Peirson Frank's engineering experience, both military and civilian, would be called upon as the threat loomed ever larger. Luckily for London, the right man was in the right place at the worst of times.

## Low Ground

Mindful of the increased threat of flooding that an all-out war would bring and well aware of the significant investments being discussed by London Transport to make the Underground safe, Peirson Frank continued making his own plans. A conference had been convened in the aftermath of the 1928 disaster 'to consider steps to obviate any reoccurrence', as Dr Carlsson-Hyslop's research shows. At this time, LCC was responsible for setting the level to which London's flood defences should be raised, but it was the owners of the riverside properties who bore the costs of such heightenings, a situation with which the many riparian boroughs took issue. It was felt that more research was required to ascertain the causes and potential frequency of such exceptionally high tides, and therefore what the optimum height of river walls required should be and what the consequent cost might be. Yet such studies were not regarded by national government as requiring funding by them. Not for the first time, there was simply no consensus on central, regional and local government views, even on such a key issue as flood defence. The deadlock was only broken by Peirson Frank himself when, in 1937, the Chief Engineer agreed to fund the research on behalf of LCC, given the pressing need for the study and the 'continued refusal of HM Government to defray' the costs required; flood defence was therefore still clearly perceived by them as a local and not a national issue.

The study commissioned by LCC involved the Liverpool Tidal Institute (now the National Oceanographic Centre), in association with the Meteorological Office and the Admiralty's Hydrographic Department. As shall be shown, the Chief Engineer's contacts with these agencies played a role in the development of the Thames-Flood Prevention Emergency Repairs programme.

Peirson Frank's next action was to ascertain the scale of the threat to London, and so a detailed survey was undertaken of LCC's river frontage. This study identified all locations where the ground surface immediately behind the river wall was less than +14ft OD (i.e. some 4.3m above Ordnance Datum) and thus vulnerable to inundation at exceptionally high tides. The river defences themselves were supposed to be brought up to a height of at least 17ft 6in above OD, referred to as the 'standard level', although this was itself nearly 1ft (0.3m) lower than the 'exceptional' floodwaters of 1928.

The survey was then extended landwards away from the river wall to map the extent of all ground below that height. Thus the weakest points in London's river defences were all systematically plotted out, perhaps for the first time. Alarmingly, many problem areas were identified and these were graded I, II or III (major, intermediate and relatively 'minor'), depending on the vulnerability of existing defences as well as the size or importance of the area that might flood if a breach occurred.

Bermondsey fared the worst with eight Grade I, eleven Grade II and three Grade III sites; Battersea was not far behind with eight Grade I and two Grade III sites. The next two most vulnerable boroughs were Poplar with six Grade I, two Grade II and seven Grade III, and then Greenwich with four Grade I, two Grade II and three Grade III sites. As for the rest of the south bank, Lambeth had one Grade I, two Grade II and one Grade III, while Southwark had six Grade III sites. On the opposite shore, Fulham had one Grade II, Westminster one Grade I, and Stepney one Grade II and five Grade III sites (Flood Prevention & River Defences 1939–45: Correspondence files LCC/CE/WAR/02/011).

On 12 October 1939, the Chief Engineer then wrote to each of these nine riparian boroughs explaining that

> LCC has statutory powers to ensure that defences against flooding from the Thames ... are maintained in a satisfactory condition ... defences adequate in times of peace may not be capable of resisting aerial bombardment, and an investigation has recently been made of the protective works on the banks of the Thames...with the object of ascertaining where breaches might occur, and of assessing risk of damage in each case.

He then listed each potential danger site in each borough so that remedial action could be targeted on the most vulnerable. Taking into account the distribution and concentrations of the majority of the Grade I sites, he proposed that four 'Thames-Flood-Prevention' depots be established. Each was carefully located to be close to the most vulnerable areas and also to take advantage of good road links within the boroughs. They were also situated near bridges or tunnels under the Thames as well as access to wharves for transport on the river if required. Thus, in the event of any one depot being unable to function, one of the others could cover for it.

One of the four teams was stationed at a depot in the north-west corner of Battersea Park to deal with incidents in Battersea and Lambeth as well as across the river in Fulham and Westminster. Another was on the Isle of Dogs

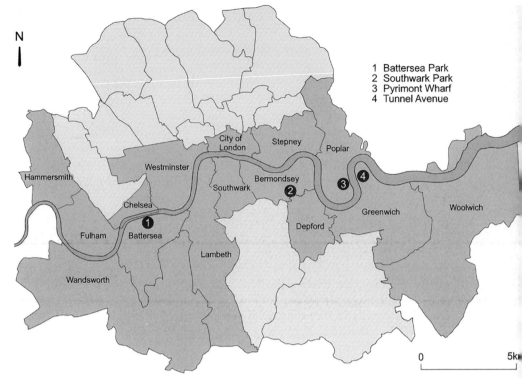

1 Battersea Park
2 Southwark Park
3 Pyrimont Wharf
4 Tunnel Avenue

Base camp. All four depots for LCC's rapid-response units were in areas vulnerable to flooding: (1) Stoneyard, Battersea Park; (2) China Hall Gate, Southwark Park; (3) Pyrimont Wharf, Millwall; and (4) Tunnel Avenue, Greenwich. The named Thames-side boroughs are those that were under the aegis of LCC in 1940. (© *Museum of London Archaeology*)

at Pyrimont Wharf for Wapping, Limehouse, Stepney and Poplar, with a third at Tunnel Avenue, Greenwich covering incidents from Deptford to Woolwich. The fourth was in the south-east corner of Southwark Park for Rotherhithe, Bermondsey and Southwark.

Large stocks of earth and sand, sandbags, tarpaulins, timber and tools would be stored here, secured within a locked compound. The importance of such well-managed facilities is highlighted in a report from the City of Westminster to the Chief Engineer regarding an additional temporary store of 9,000 sandbags held by that borough in Millbank Gardens. The conditions here were less than ideal and the sandbags had rotted, partially as a result of inadequate protection from the weather, coupled with 'interference by children'. Such a fate could not befall the sandbags stored by the T-F team.

In addition to their all-weather, child-proof storage facilities, there would be mess rooms for T-F staff, an air-raid shelter and an office which, it was noted, was fitted with a telephone. Lorries would have to be bought and maintained, and a fleet of barges hired at a cost of £42 per week. In quiet times, the depots would be manned by a labourer, a lorry driver and a night watchman, but during a period of prolonged air-raids, the staff would increase

Roadworks: every borough had to keep its roads clear of bomb debris, get bomb craters filled in and keep traffic moving. Gangs of labourers, often too old for military service such as those here in Upper Thames Street, were employed for this task. They were also seconded by LCC to work for the Thames-Flood rapid-response teams. (*LMA: © Cross & Tibbs Collection 35614*)

to one engineer, a foreman, two labourers and two lorry drivers. To this core complement, whenever the air-raid sirens actually sounded, a team of four-teen labourers would be added, men drawn from the local borough's road repair gangs: these men would serve for the duration of the raid before being stood down at the all-clear. They were thus 'volunteered' for active service.

## High Tide

To these careful preparations, another letter with a crucial calendar was added. This was circulated to the boroughs on 13 May 1940, and listed the dates and estimated times of forty-four dangerously high spring tides antici-pated that year; the tidal information was provided by the Admiralty's Hydro-graphic Office. The T-F team now knew precisely where and precisely when London would be at its most vulnerable to flooding. Taken together, if these two documents – LCC's survey and the Admiralty's tide tables – fell into enemy hands, it could have proved catastrophic: what if the Luftwaffe had chosen to concentrate their HE (high-explosive) bombs on the weakest sections of the river wall just one or two hours before an exceptionally high tide? Well aware of the dreadful significance of this information, the tide charts were sent to just one named officer in each borough, but only after the name, address and nationality of that individual had been security-vetted.

Having now checked the pattern and timing of the raids that followed, it can be seen that the Luftwaffe did not fully appreciate the significance of those very particular dates and times. Although the bomber pilots certainly appreciated the navigational value of a full moon, very few major raids actually coincided with the very highest tides; a great but unrecorded relief to London. This helps to explain why the work of the T-F unit went virtually unnoticed; the Chief Engineer knew how vulnerable London was to a severe raid mounted just before a high spring tide. With hindsight, we can now surmise that the Luftwaffe was less well informed. Had they realized, then presumably they would have exploited the situation to ill effect. LCC's policy of deliberately not discussing or widely reporting any of the river wall breaches definitely saved lives.

*Chapter Three*

# Come Hell and High Water:
# 1940–45

## The Gathering Storm

During 1940, with the fall of France, Operation DYNAMO at Dunkirk, and the Battle of Britain being fought overhead, real concern was mounting regarding the reality of an enemy invasion. Its code-name was Operation SEALION: the German 6th, 9th and 16th armies would be launched across the Channel to land at a range of sites from Ramsgate to Lyme Regis. Air superiority was required to ensure the success of this enterprise, but the RAF fought hard to deny the Nazi war machine that key component; by September 1940 they had succeeded and the threatened invasion was postponed. The Luftwaffe then changed tactics and moved from attacking airfields towards the carpet-bombing of economic and civilian targets. Shouldering the burden of this new phase of the war was thus shared not just by 'The Few' but by the many, including the non-combatant civilian population of London.

## Into Battle

However, would widespread flooding be added to the coming ordeal by fire? LCC's serious planning for flood prevention in anticipation of the unpredictability of total war had already begun by 1939. A hand-written sheet estimating the costs required to set up and run the four Thames-Flood depots came up with the figure of £16,484, which was rounded up to £18,000. It also included an estimate of the anticipated workload. In the event of air-raids on London and consequent damage to the river defences, it was suggested that, by the end of the war, there could be up to a hundred 'ineffective alarms' at £15 per time, but some six major 'breaches', the temporary repairs for each one costing some £30 a time.

How accurate would that projection be? The detailed preparations made by LCC were, unfortunately, put to the test, starting all too violently with the massive air-raids of 7–8 September 1940. Some 40 serious and 1,000 'smaller' fires were started, causing widespread devastation and 2,000 civilian fatalities or major injuries. All of the emergency services were stretched to breaking-point and beyond that night; the damage and destruction inflicted by the

Baptism of fire. St Katharine Docks, September 1940: the Auxiliary Fire Service rises to the challenge. (*Mary Evans Picture Library: © London Fire Brigade 11966765*)

Luftwaffe was worse, far worse, than anybody had imagined or the authorities had estimated.

In the first three days of the Blitz, all four Thames-Flood Depots had been in action, repairing river walls near burning gas-holders, railway yards, busy wharves and even on the Victoria Embankment. It was clear that the initial projections were woefully inaccurate, since the Thames-Flood teams already had more than six major breaches to contend with after the first major raids. By mid-September, Peirson Frank was reviewing and revising the situation, as indeed were all those agencies trying to cope with the ferocious carpet-bombing of such a large conurbation.

In the cold light of that September's experience, consideration was given to the use of teams with specialist heavy-lifting gear and augmenting the modest resources initially apportioned to the Thames-Flood units with parties of Royal Engineers; a gang of just seven labourers was not always sufficient to deal with the worst of the riverside problems caused by the Luftwaffe.

How to coordinate the work of these extra teams exercised the minds of the LCC, and a *modus operandi* was established. Among the key initiatives proposed was that five specific 'Rendezvous Points' should be established, at which a member of the T-F team would stand with a white flag for recognition (there were no street lights at night) and written directions as to where the major incident was. All the Royal Engineers had to do was get to that named rendezvous point when requested; the T-F team would take control from then on. This basic system obviated the need for complex directions to obscure wharf-side addresses being relayed over malfunctioning telephones during a heavy air-raid. One can speculate that the new system was in direct response to problems already experienced.

Another development concerned the perceived need to have teams on standby before each high spring tide, regardless of whether or not the air-raid sirens had sounded. Related to this development is a letter requesting that a despatch rider be based at Pyrimont Wharf from the blackout to the following morning during the nights that a high spring tide was anticipated to speed up communications should a flood emergency arise. Taken together, these developments all show how seriously the threat of flooding was taken, and how the scale of the raids in September had shaken all remnants of complacency from the planning machine; nothing could or should be left to chance and fire must be met with foresight.

In total, the T-F log books record that the river wall was hit some 122 times between September 1940 and March 1945. By far the most intense period for the T-F teams was the Blitz running up to May 1941, during which period some eighty incidents were dealt with in nine months. Many of these bomb strikes could have resulted in a subsequent serious flood event, but none did. The T-F's own assessment of this period records nearly a third of the incidents were seen as 'major'; these were all plotted on a plan at a scale of 2in to 1 mile (c. 1:30,000).

One of the worst raids for the T-F unit was unquestionably the eight-hour assault on 10/11 May 1941; Hitler's farewell gift to London before he turned his attentions to the Eastern Front. Some 800 tons of high explosives and 100,000 incendiaries rained down on London, killing 1,436 Londoners. On that one night alone, the T-F log books record some twenty separate incidents, involving all four depots working flat out. A report written later that year notes the lack of reliable transport. Four out of the six lorries then used by one of the T-F units were either broken down or were too fire-damaged to use, a comment reminding us that the unit had actually been working during the raids and not just after the all-clear.

The intermittent raiding suffered by London in the second half of 1941 and throughout 1942 was minor by comparison, with 'only' fifteen incidents recorded, although several of these were a major cause of concern at the time. The return of large waves of bombers for the 'Little Blitz' in early 1943 was met with a battle-hardened response and much improved AA defences; again, just fifteen incidents were recorded by the T-F teams.

In 1944, just as London thought it had the measure of the enemy as the Allies started the fight-back in Normandy, a new weapon appeared in the sky. Or perhaps it would be more accurate to say exploded without warning. The cause of the incident that blew up the Grove Road Bridge at Bow was initially reported as 'an aeroplane which must have burst in the air': the government was reluctant to admit that London was now the target of rocket attacks.

The V-1 (or 'doodlebug') makes its first appearance in the T-F log books on 18 June, when a PAC (Pilotless Air Craft) is recorded as hitting Caledonia Wharf in Deptford Creek. Fourteen more hit the river wall over the next three months, often with devastating results, while another hit Charing Cross Bridge.

The Allied forces destroyed the launch sites for these weapons as they fought their way across northern Europe. However, no sooner had the doodlebug menace been more or less mastered than Londoners had to face an even worse fate. From September 1944 the threat was from V-2 rockets, dispatched from mobile launchers to arrive without any warning and at supersonic speed. Initially, the official response was one of denial: Churchill himself did not admit publicly that London was under attack from these deadly rockets until 10 November, two months later. In total, some 1,358 were launched against London, killing 2,754 of its civilian population. There seemed to be no defence. For example, it rendered obsolete the complex early-warning system set up to ensure that the Underground railway tunnels under the Thames could be closed off to secure the network from widespread flooding.

The official view of the effect this rocket bombardment would have was also not shared with the populace. Once again, secrecy was the watchword as detailed preparations were put in hand to evacuate 250,000 people between July and September 1945, a complex programme involving trains, trams and buses. In the event, the Allies battled their way into Germany overrunning the rocket sites, and by 28 March 1945 the V-2 attack was over. Large consignments of rocket parts were captured and shipped to the United States, along with 126 members of the design team, including Wernher von Braun and Walter Dornberger. Rather than being tried for their many war crimes, their expertise was then exploited by NASA's space programme to put a man on the moon.

As for the T-F teams in 1945, it was another incident at Deptford that heralded the arrival of those awful weapons on 17 March. However, as time ran out for the Nazi war machine, there were only two more V-2 incidents recorded in the T-F log books. The last entry concerns the strike at Ovex Wharf in Poplar on 24 March 1945 (TF121), when a rocket demolished the wharf buildings and damaged the frontage next to the slipway. The blast debris blocking the breach was not cleared away until 21 June, long after the VE Day celebrations. Only then could the T-F team set up their last temporary flood defence, a final wall of 400 sandbags.

## *Modus Operandi*

To keep pace with the Blitz on the river, a well-practised *modus operandi* was rapidly developed by the T-F teams. Having received a report that there was a bomb strike on the waterfront, perhaps from the local ARP team or the River Police, a T-F engineer would get to the site – in the dark during a raid – to ascertain the damage. It is clear that he had detailed knowledge of the area and was armed with maps and plans, since the precise heights of the river wall and of any secondary lines of flood defence in the immediate vicinity is regularly recorded in the log books. If the flood defences had withstood the

Night watch: all through the Blitz a network of observers noted where bombs fell and where fires were started in order to inform the relevant rapid-response teams.
(© *Mary Evans Picture Library 10534649*)

Mass observation: many observation posts were constructed in and around London. This one, overlooking the Thames near Woolwich Arsenal, was recorded seventy-five years after its construction. (© *TDP, N. Cohen*)

strike, then the matter was briefly noted and no further action taken by the T-F team. If, however, there was a problem, then his incident report would receive a T-F number (e.g. TF01), and be relayed to the appropriate depot by phone – long before the age of the mobile – by land line, if one could be found in working order. If the lines were down, then the message was delivered by hand on foot, by bicycle or motor bike. The rapid-response team would then load the lorry and drive off to the site.

The repair programme usually had three, sometimes four, stages. First came the 'emergency repair'. Once the fires had been extinguished, casualties rescued and any unexploded ordnance dealt with, a temporary dam was constructed by the T-F team from whatever was to hand (often a combination of sandbags and bomb-blast debris). It would be piled up to the required height of the standard level for the area to secure the bomb crater, damaged parapet or river wall breach against the next high tide. Such work was often begun at night, during the air-raid.

The quantity of debris produced by a collapsed warehouse, coupled with its charred contents, could provide a substantial obstacle to the rising tide; there are several instances noted in the T-F log books that detailed repair work could not be commenced until the site had been cleared. In the case of

Communications network. During the Blitz, vital information was passed swiftly to teams such as the Thames-Flood units and the AFS from local control centres manned throughout each and every raid. (© *Mary Evans Picture Library 10793366*)

First responders: the AFS and rescue teams have urgent work to do before the T-F team can assess the damage to the river wall. (*Mary Evans Picture Library: © London Fire Brigade 10794927*)

How bad is the breach? Thames-Flood engineers personally investigated each incident, on land or (in this case) by boat, to see how serious the damage was and to plan accordingly. (© *LMA: TDP, P. Kennedy 12990995*)

Emergency repairs: any available debris was piled up around the edge of the crater as a protective embankment to secure the site before the next high tide. (© *LMA: TDP, P. Kennedy*)

Brandram's Wharf Rotherhithe (TF40), for example, the pile of bomb-blast debris served as the river defence from 29 December 1940 until 7 July 1941.

As soon as was practicable, the T-F team began the second phase of their work, the so-called 'temporary repair'. This often involved the laying of many tiers of sandbags or concrete bagwork (e.g. TF13b, TF19, TF24, TF34, TF47, TF114, TF118), sometimes laid in a gently-sloping pitched wall (e.g. TF11, TF13, TF16). Depending on the size of the breach, this work could take a few days or a few weeks. Both these initial stages of work were undertaken and paid for out of the T-F budget, and thus the number of sandbags and man hours expended are listed in the accounts.

According to today's flood resilience team, the Environment Agency, two people are needed to fill each 15kg sandbag (unless a holding frame is used), and it can take up to one hour to fill just twelve of them manually. A good grade of sharp sand is preferable, and the bags need to be carefully stacked and trodden into place to exclude the air and ensure that each course is level. Large walls usually incorporate bags laid like bricks, in alternate courses of headers and stretchers (widthwise and lengthwise), with the mouths of the bags facing inwards. Free-standing walls built in this fashion would have a base three times the width of their height. Once the effort and expertise required to build an effective sandbag wall are understood, then the instances of the superb examples of precision sandbagging undertaken by the T-F team can be appreciated: put bluntly, a badly-built river defence would simply not

Temporary repairs: a well-laid bank of sandbags was the preferred option for a river defence until a more permanent solution could be devised. (© *LMA: TDP, P. Kennedy TF66-1299a*)

work when pitted against the rising tide, and these 'temporary' defences had to serve for many months, often several years. The evidence suggested by the records pictured and listed in the log books shows that London's 'temporary' defences were indeed fit for purpose. This was a tribute to the engineers who designed them and the conscientious teams that filled all those many bags and carefully laid them.

The next stage, when things went according to plan, would be the 'permanent repair'. There was often a delay before this phase could begin, however, as it was not funded by the T-F unit but by the site owner as and when the required resources could be found. Such work might therefore be started many months after the initial strike. While waiting for the reinstatement to begin, the T-F team kept a meticulous eye on such protracted programmes. They were not their financial responsibility, but they could become their next problem should the temporary sandbag wall collapse, undoing all their good work. Such continuous scrutiny was certainly necessary. At Odessa Wharf, Rotherhithe (TF57), for example, the temporary bagwork required frequent replacement; here the stated cause was 'children'. On several of the other sites where it is recorded that the bagwork was repeatedly 'disturbed', it may well be that local residents, living in bomb-shattered housing, found other uses for the seemingly limitless supply of sandbags piled on the riverfront. The T-F engineers therefore regularly re-inspected all their sites to check on the effectiveness of the temporary repairs and the progress of reinstatement.

'Permanent Repairs' were usually to a design drawn up by the T-F engineers – or at least to their specifications – and the log books often record

Permanent repairs: if the waterfront property owner could afford the required timber, brick or concrete, then the breached river wall could be reinstated. (© *TDP, P. Kennedy TF59*)

the dates on which work finally started and when it was eventually completed. The incident would then be signed off with a date, a large red tick and some relief. However, the log books rarely record what materials were used for those final repairs, and thus it falls to modern-day archaeologists to catalogue whether they were of timber, brick, masonry (e.g. TF16), shuttered concrete (TF11), or a combination of materials (TF59).

Progress was not always that straightforward, however, and an intervening phase of 'semi-permanent repairs' made a regular appearance in the schedules. This provided a more robust if rough and ready solution to the challenge of keeping the river out. These works were sometimes done by the depots, sometimes in tandem with the site owners. The term 'semi-permanent' used by the T-F team obviously implies that a more aesthetic refurbishment would be undertaken at a future date when time and money were in better supply;

interestingly, some of these 'semi-permanents' are still visible today (e.g. TF49, TF60).

For this class of repair, the techniques and materials varied nearly as much as the locations. Breaches in the river wall itself below the level of high tide were normally rebuilt in brick (e.g. TF39) or concrete (e.g. TF54). Where the lower levels of a substantial waterfront warehouse also incorporated the riverside wall, a range of repair options was possible. The burned-out façade, if still structurally intact, could be retained, but with its lower openings either bricked up or concreted in (e.g. TF72, TF77, TF99). If the building had been demolished – either by the Luftwaffe or by the Royal Engineers – then a new parapet wall could be created from the footings of the warehouse, backed with a mix of bomb debris and concrete; this was a common solution (e.g. TF38, TF49, TF57, TF79, TF80, TF87, TF95, TF96).

Edwin Trout of the Concrete Society has kindly added the following comments. He suggests that such waterfront repairs would have been conducted quickly and with whatever concrete was available in wartime. Since the usual binder was Portland cement, which is hydraulic, the concrete would set under water, but the repair team would have to avoid wash-out and guard against saturation. A rapid-setting concrete might have been preferred such as calcium aluminate cement, which was produced at that time by Lafarge Aluminates, based on the Thames at Grays. A new 'quick-setting and quick-hardening cement' for war work was launched by the Cement Marketing Co. in May 1941, called '417' cement. Since its initial setting time was twenty minutes with a final set in sixty minutes, it would have been ideal for work between low and high water (Edwin Trout pers. comm.).

Another initiative concerned the timber 'movable dams' (sometimes called tide-boards) that slotted into doorways, windows and at the tops of river stairs to bring the height of such features safely above the standard level. Several of these dams were burned or otherwise damaged during the raids, or removed and not replaced. A programme was thus set up to convert these 'movable' features into more permanent, fixed assets in the more vulnerable locations, using fixed timber, brick or concrete (e.g. TF75, TF76, TF81, TF82, TF83, TF86, TF89, TF104).

On more open waterfront sites, construction, repair, raising or strengthening of the parapet was required. It should be stressed that the ground level behind such apparently slight walls was often below the required standard level, in some areas by an alarmingly significant amount. Thus damage to the parapet posed a real threat to low-lying London, potentially as dangerous as a breach to the river wall itself. As a consequence, much time and effort was expended on their maintenance and repair. On the Victoria Embankment, for example, the dressed granite parapet was strengthened with metal dowels on

Rough and ready: coarse-mix shuttered concrete repairs on Bermondsey waterfront still visible thirty years after the Blitz. (© *LMA 281214*)

On the level: riverside parapet formed by footings of a demolished bomb-damaged warehouse, thickened with concrete and raised to a new safe 'standard level' above the height of the highest anticipated tides. Puddle Dock, Blackfriars in 1952: note the incomplete Bankside Power Station (Tate Modern) across the river. (© *Museum of London 818147*)

the riverward side (e.g. TF05) and with concrete buttresses or piers on the landward side (e.g. TF60). Concrete was widely used elsewhere too, although in less prestigious situations a newly-aligned wall was set back from the original frontage where space allowed (e.g. TF21a, TF25, TF25a, TF28, TF40, TF62, TF70). One of these newly-built parapet walls had a sandbag core within a bomb-debris shell, then sealed by concrete (TF116). The secondary line of flood defences, often set back further inland, might be brick-built (e.g. TF91).

Thus the work of the T-F service was clearly a long-drawn-out affair. It started with initial flood-risk surveys, then the setting up of the secondary defences. Next came the bomb strikes and the consequent emergency works, followed up by the temporary and semi-permanent repair phases, all of which took time to implement, as did the protracted monitoring programme for these and the associated permanent works. Each single 'incident' therefore encapsulates many weeks' work. By the end of the war, the Pyrimont Wharf team handled some forty incidents, including both the first and the last listed in the log books. Battersea dealt with thirty, while Southwark and Greenwich dealt with some twenty each. In the event, the Tunnel Avenue depot was mothballed in October 1941, leaving just three depots in operation from then until hostilities ended.

## Closure

Although Battersea Park and Pyrimont Wharf were closed by 17 May 1945, the Southwark Park depot was retained a little longer to renew a number of temporary flood defences constructed on sites where the owners or occupiers had been unable to initiate more permanent reinstatement. That work was completed by June 1945, when a memo from the coordinating officer recorded the closing of all the depots, and thus formally brought to an end the Thames-Flood Prevention Emergency Repair Service.

Although the depots had been decommissioned and the unit largely disbanded by the end of 1945, LCC's engineer's department continued to deal with the long trail of paperwork and the restitution costs that resulted from the 'Thames-Flood' work. In 1947, for example, discussions were still continuing regarding the cost of removing elements of the secondary line of flood defences, constructed as a precautionary measure in 1940. One such scheme was the removal of debris tipped into Shadwell Old Basin at a cost of £1,524, a bill finally passed for payment on 3 March 1947. Of rather more significance is that the T-F engineers themselves who continued to work for the LCC Chief Engineer's department did not relinquish their T-F responsibilities or their scrutiny of the T-F log books after 1945: as late as 1946, checks were being made on the quality of the 'permanent' repairs still being undertaken on the last of the bomb-damaged river walls in Bermondsey. The T-F log book entry for the incident at the Montreal Granary site (TF117) finally signs it off two years and three months later on 11 November 1946, which, appropriately enough, was Armistice Day.

5.

PART TWO

# THE RAPID-RESPONSE TEAMS
# IN ACTION

*Chapter Four*

# Pyrimont Wharf:
# The Millwall Depot

The Pyrimont Wharf depot was on the eastern side of the Isle of Dogs at the end of Saunderness Road. It was north of Plymouth Wharf, south of Dudgeon's Wharf and almost opposite the Greenwich Tunnel Avenue depot on the other side of the river. This particularly busy T-F team attended incidents in Wapping, Limehouse, Stepney and Poplar, boroughs which between them included six very vulnerable low-lying sites. The designated rendezvous point, where a detachment of Royal Engineers or a team with heavy-lifting gear would be met, was at the north entrance to the Blackwall Tunnel, in the East India Dock Road.

The Pyrimont Wharf team's own baptism of fire began in the aftermath of the 7 September conflagration. Bombs fell to the north, west and south of them, but the depot was spared. This was the night that saw the Royal Docks ablaze: the population of Silvertown, cut off by a ring of fire to the north, had to be evacuated by the industry of LCC's four Woolwich ferries, *Will Crooks*, *John Benn*, *Squires* and *Gordon*. They steamed back and forth across the river, oblivious to the bombing and the oil slicks burning on the water until this mini-Dunkirk had been successfully completed. As for the T-F team, they were attending incidents at a gas works, a lead works and a working wharf, a fair cross-section of the environment they would be trying to protect for the rest of the war.

In February 1941, Peirson Frank wrote to the Pyrimont depot in response to a request from the working party for the provision of overalls, as the team had just been working on what was left of an oil wharf. One can but sympathize with such a request, since it shows that the labourers were expected to work in the mud, rubble and sundry contaminants in their own clothes. However, the Chief Engineer was unmoved and argued that the working party was on that particular site for 'only three days'. He did agree, however, that in future he would pay them extra – so-called 'dirty money' – 'at such times as you may consider the nature of the site or work render such a procedure justifiable.' It would be interesting to note which of the smoke-blackened bomb-sites on the battered and polluted wharves of Millwall were considered 'clean'.

## Incidents Attended by the T-F Millwall Team

| | | |
|---|---|---|
| TF01 | Gas Works, Leven Road, Poplar | September 1940 |
| TF02 | Millwall Lead Works, Poplar | September 1940 |
| TF06 | Bullivant's Wharf, Poplar | September 1940 |
| TF07 | North Woolwich Station, Poplar | September 1940 |
| TF14 | Union Wharf, Poplar | October 1940 |
| TF18 | Slipway Wharf, Poplar | October 1940 |
| TF26 | Commercial Gas Co., Poplar | November 1940 |
| TF30 | Rose's Wharf, Limehouse | November 1940 |
| TF31 | Winkley's Wharf, Poplar | December 1940 |
| TF32 | Bridge Wharf, Poplar | December 1940 |
| TF34 | Samuda's Wharf, Poplar | December 1940 |
| TF37 | Grosvenor Wharf, Poplar | December 1940 |
| TF38 | Black Eagle Wharf, Limehouse | December 1940 |
| TF39 | Hermitage Wharf, Limehouse | December 1940 |
| TF43 | LMS A Dock, Poplar | January 1941 |
| TF44 | LMS A Dock, Poplar | January 1941 |
| TF45 | LMS B Dock, Poplar | January 1941 |
| TF46 | LMS B Dock, Poplar | no date, presumably January 1941 |
| TF50 | Rose's Wharf, Poplar | March 1941 |
| TF51 | St Andrew's Wharf, Poplar | March 1941 |
| TF52 | Fenner's Wharf, Poplar | March 1941 |
| TF53 | Anchor Wharf, Limehouse | March 1941 |
| TF54 | Hutching's Wharf, Poplar | March 1941 |
| TF55 | Dux Chemical Works, River Lea | March 1941 |
| TF56 | Lea Foundry, River Lea | March 1941 |
| TF65 | Millwall Wharf, Poplar | April 1941 |
| TF66 | Glengall Wharf, Poplar | May 1941 |
| TF67 | Union Wharf, Poplar | May 1941 |
| TF74 | Watson's Wharf, Limehouse | May 1941 |
| TF75 | Upper Standard Wharf, Limehouse | May 1941 |
| TF76 | Standard Sufferance Wharf, Limehouse | May 1941 |
| TF77 | British & Foreign Wharf, Stepney | May 1941 |
| TF81 | St Helen's Wharf, Limehouse | May 1941 |
| TF83 | Thorpe's Wharf, Limehouse | May 1941 |
| TF84 | St George's Wharf, Poplar | March 1941 |
| TF94 | Eagle Wharf, Limehouse | May 1941? |
| TF89 | Aberdeen Wharf, Poplar | September 1941 |
| TF90 | Otis Wharf, River Lea | September 1941? |
| TF91 | Old Ford Road, River Lea | September 1941? |
| TF103 | St Andrew's Wharf, Poplar | February 1944 |
| TF105 | Napier Yard, Poplar | June 1944 |
| TF120 | Leamouth, River Lea | March 1945 |
| TF121 | Ovex Wharf, Poplar | March 1945 |

Satanic mills: Thames-side wharves were crowded with industries dealing with toxic and flammable products. This posed additional problems for fire-fighters and for Thames-Flood teams working on sites such as Winkley's Wharf, with its fuel storage tanks shown here under fire. (*Mary Evans Picture Library:* © *London Fire Brigade 10793950*)

Risk assessment: fire-fighters at Winkley's Wharf during the Blitz; note the drums of paraffin wax waiting to ignite. (*Mary Evans Picture Library* © *London Fire Brigade 10793996*)

# Selected Incidents

### TF02 Millwall Lead Works (St David's Wharf)

One of the first incidents dealt with by the Millwall team was reported to them by the River Police at Wapping. A bomb with a delayed timer penetrated Lock & Lancaster's wharf, destroying the timber cladding on the river wall, and then exploded later on the foreshore. Some 200 sandbags were packed around the edge of the crater until more permanent repairs to the timberwork could be installed some six months later in February 1941.

### TF06 Bullivant Wharf

[Incorrectly transcribed as Barnard's Wharf in the T-F log book.] Bullivant Wharf suffered an infamous disaster in 1941 when a direct hit on a warehouse with a public shelter in the basement killed forty-four people. Prior to that incident, that wharf and the neighbouring Stronghold Wharf were wire rope manufactories. On 15 September 1940, a bomb demolished the waterfront buildings and part of the timber-faced quay. The doorway in the shell of the building was bricked up to form a second line of defence and sandbags were placed around the edge of the crater. Scouring continued, however, and a more secure temporary repair was instigated on 18 September; the photo above was taken in March 1941 and shows 1,000 sandbags carefully laid in tiers. A more permanent repair in timber was completed later that year, between May and July.

T-F incident no. 6, Bullivant's (Barnard's) Wharf: Stronghold and Bullivant's wharves were wire rope manufactories in 1937. (© *Museum of London: PLA Collection, 322024*)

Bullivant's Wharf: following a bomb strike in 1940, the subsequent temporary repair required 1,000 sandbags, as photographed here in March 1941. (© *LMA: TDP, P. Kennedy 281214*)

## TF31 Winkley's Wharf

On 8 December 1940, a bomb destroyed 40ft of the wharf's timber facing down to foreshore level as a contemporary photo below shows. It took a seven-man team nearly four days to build a defensive wall set back from the

T-F incident no. 31, Winkley's Wharf: established by Mark Winkley in the 1890s, it was principally an oil storage facility in 1937. (© *Museum of London: PLA Collection 322032*)

Winkley's Wharf: showing oil drums in the foreground ready to explode in 1940.
(*Mary Evans Picture Library: © London Fire Brigade 10793951*)

Fire-boat illuminated by flames: dispersing burning oil pouring into the river from Winkley's Wharf in 1940. (*Mary Evans Picture Library: © London Fire Brigade 10793997*)

Bomb damage to Winkley's Wharf: photographed in December 1940.
(© *LMA: TDP, P. Kennedy TF031 1160*)

damaged frontage, using 950 sandbags. Those bags secured the site for nearly
six months while permanent reinstatement was planned and installed. This
was in the form of new timber-faced frontage; a contemporary photo shows
the pile-driver used to drive the uprights into position in May 1941.

Repairs to Winkley's Wharf: repairs to the river wall were undertaken after the bomb strikes.
Subsequently more permanent repairs began, in the form of this timber-faced frontage, photographed during construction in May 1941. (© *LMA: TDP, P. Kennedy TF031*)

T-F incident no. 51, St Andrew's Wharf. By 1937, the Thames Oil Wharf Company was storing petroleum here. (© *Museum of London: PLA Collection 322050*)

### TF51 St Andrew's

Fire destroyed the buildings as well as a 30ft length of the timber-clad river-front at St Andrew's Wharf (owned by the Thames Oil Wharf Co.) on 19 March 1941. The loose ground behind the frontage began scouring immediately. The situation was temporarily contained by a wall of 630 sandbags until new piles could be driven and timber cladding installed by September 1941.It took a seven-man team nearly four days to build a defensive wall set back from the damaged frontage, using 950 sandbags.

Following a bomb strike in 1941 that destroyed the timber facing of St Andrew's Wharf, the unstable core of the waterfront was exposed. Extensive scouring by the tidal river began progressively enlarging the crater, exposing the subsurface pipework for the fuel tanks as shown here. (© *LMA: TDP, P. Kennedy TF0311233*)

T-F incident no. 66, Glengall Wharf. This site, also owned by the Thames Oil Wharf Company, had a vulnerable timber-clad river frontage as shown in this 1937 image.
(© *Museum of London: PLA Collection 322029*)

## TF66 Glengall Wharf

During the heavy raid on 10 May 1941, the timber-clad frontage of Glengall Wharf and the neighbouring Union Wharf were badly damaged by a bomb that left a 90ft crater on the waterfront. The emergency repairs shown in a contemporary photo consisted simply of debris piled up around the edge of

Glengall Wharf was one of many that suffered in the raids of 10/11 May 1941: this photo shows mounds of debris hastily piled up by the T-F team on the edge of the bomb crater to contain the next high tide. (© *LMA: TDP, P. Kennedy TF661294*)

Work begins on foundations for 'temporary' repairs at Glengall Wharf to prevent further scouring. (© *LMA: TDP, P. Kennedy TF661295*)

The T-F engineer oversees the construction of the footings for the sandbag wall.
(© *LMA: TDP, P. Kennedy TF661295*)

Superb example of a carefully-engineered sandbag repair work at Glengall Wharf. Although this was classed as a 'temporary' solution, it served as the flood defence for eighteen months. (© *LMA: TDP, P. Kennedy TF661296*)

Modern view of Glengall Wharf, now largely defended by sheet piling. The section that has additional foreshore piling is close to the site of the 1941 bomb strike. (© *TDP*)

the crater, topped with a single row of sandbags. The next phase, the temporary repair, comprised a reinforced pitched wall of no less than 6,680 sandbags, supported by a foundation formed by a line of driven piles standing 5ft above the foreshore, concreted in. The work took over 900 man hours, from 16 May to 29 August 1941, and is recorded in a contemporary photograph.

A timely T-F inspection of the site just a year later showed that the bottom of the wall was disintegrating, requiring remedial attention. The owner of the wharf was immediately approached to push ahead with the permanent repairs, but these only commenced on 15 March 1943 (TF1002/43). Thus the 'temporary' repair shown here lasted for some eighteen months.

### TF94 Eagle Wharf

The image of the site in the summer of 1937 perfectly captures the character of pre-war Wapping. It shows Eagle Wharf where, among the barges and busy warehouses, three local kids are playing cricket on the foreshore, having enjoyed a swim in the none-too-inviting river. It wasn't just the built fabric of maritime London that the Blitz swept away but, for better or worse, much of its social context too.

The photo taken on 14 March 1941 shows how effective a mixture of a collapsed warehouse and its contents can be in the formation of an emergency

T-F incident no. 94, Eagle Wharf. This evocative image of Eagle and Baltic wharves in 1937 shows that cargoes were still being handled, working directly with lighters berthed on the adjacent foreshore. Local children play cricket, while a mudlarker stoops to see what the tide brought in. The Blitz destroyed not just the economy but also the social and cultural context captured here. (© *Museum of London: PLA Collection 321972*)

Collapsed wall and contents of the Eagle Wharf warehouse form a ready-made emergency dam that prevented flooding of the hinterland after the 1941 bomb strike.
(© *LMA: TDP, P. Kennedy TF941409*)

dam. It also shows the difficulties faced by the T-F team trying to work on riverside bomb sites without access to heavy-lifting gear. It was not until the site had been cleared in October six months later that the cracked river wall could be properly examined. A defence of 650 sandbags was then laid across the back of the site, with a moveable timber dam in the centre for vehicular access.

A later inspection of the wall revealed some 'disturbance', and the missing bags were then replaced in June 1942 with concrete 'dowelled together with rods obtained from scrap dumps'. This solution seems to have worked until the permanent repairs commenced in January 1945. These involved the reuse of as much of the sound river wall as possible, patched in concrete and otherwise made good. The result can still be seen below the railings that front the small park that now occupies the site of those demolished warehouses.

### TF105 Napier's Yard

The T-F log book for 21 June records that a PAC (now better known as a doodlebug or V-1 rocket) demolished the timber cladding and 45ft of the timber capping at Napier's Yard. No temporary works were undertaken by the T-F team as the owners claimed that they were already planning to replace the entire frontage in this area. The inspectors visited the site again in July, but found no progress had been made. However, the work did eventually begin, with the timber cladding reinstated by 28 August and the timber capping two months later.

Although all signs of that timberwork have now disappeared behind steel sheet piling, the Thames Discovery Programme team nevertheless did find direct evidence of this incident: the crater formed by the rocket when it hit the

T-F incident no. 105, Napier/Burrells Wharf. This section of Millwall's waterfront had many uses, from shipbuilding to the manufacture of dyes and pigments for paint in 1937. (© *Museum of London: PLA Collection 322049*)

foreshore, directly in front of the river wall. By chance, the foreshore here does not comprise sands, silts and gravel, mobile materials that would not have preserved the outline of the crater for seventy years. Instead the rocket struck the solid concrete and timber slipway constructed in 1858 for the launch of Isambard Kingdom Brunel's SS *Great Eastern*. That magnificent ship, one of the greatest wonders of her age, was nevertheless dogged by ill fortune: to the catalogue of calamities that beset her before she was ignominiously broken up, we can now add that her launch site was destroyed by a doodlebug.

Crater left by a V-1 rocket that struck Burrells Wharf still visible on the foreshore. Outline preserved in shattered concrete base of slipway constructed to launch Isambard Kingdom Brunel's leviathan, the SS *Great Eastern* in 1858. The historic slipways were also recorded by the community archaeologists. (© *TDP, N. Cohen*)

# Chapter Five

# China Hall Gate:
# The Southwark Depot

The T-F team based in Southwark Park worked in an area that stretched from Rotherhithe in the east, through Bermondsey and into Southwark, as far west as Blackfriars. Their manor included a multitude of private wharves and boat-yards on the riverward side of the Surrey Docks, an area that was particularly badly hit on 7-8 September 1940. When the City of London went up in flames on 29 December that year, this T-F team also lent a hand on the river-front defences there.

They were based in Southwark Park, a desperately-needed public open space in the unhealthy and overcrowded borough of Bermondsey. However, this park, like most others, was requisitioned for war work in 1939. Some 150 trees were felled, 4 acres of allotments were laid out for food production, barrage balloons were tethered to the bandstand, communal shelters for 250 residents were dug near Jamaica Road, another area became a dump for building debris cleared from the devastated neighbourhood, and the boating lake and lido became static water reservoirs for the Fire Service. An even bigger impact was made by the large Anti-Aircraft Battery No. ZE12 that moved in, with one set of guns near the bowling green and another in The Oval cricket ground. This was manned by both regular and Home Guard units, and was later converted to rocket batteries. All this information is recorded in Pat Kingwell's admirable study of the park, but no mention is made of the Thames-Flood unit. This, it must be stressed, is no reflection on the author's research skills, but of the secrecy that surrounded T-F at the time; none of the local residents interviewed for the book ever mentioned the depot.

The unpublished records in the London Metropolitan Archives reveal that the offices and stores of Thames-Flood's Southwark team stood on the site now occupied by the Sports Centre, and shared access through the 'China Hall Gate' with the AA battery. One wonders how, at the height of the Blitz, important telephone messages were relayed by the T-F staff while a heavy barrage was being delivered. Having an AA unit next door was no guarantee of safety, however, since the park suffered several hits during the Blitz, including the destruction of the China Hall Gate entrance, an incident that presumably also impacted directly on the T-F depot.

| Incidents Attended by the T-F Southwark Team | | |
|---|---|---|
| TF09 | Horseferry Wharf, Rotherhithe | September 1940 |
| TF21/2 | Trinity & Durand's Wharves, Rotherhithe | September 1940 |
| TF23 | Shuter's Wharf, Bermondsey | May 1941 |
| TF25 | Bullivant's Wharf, Rotherhithe | September 1940 |
| TF40 | Brandram's Wharf, Rotherhithe | December 1940 |
| TF41 | Yardley's Wharf, Rotherhithe | December 1940 |
| TF47 | Danzie Wharf, Rotherhithe | February 1941 |
| TF48 | Cotton's Wharf, Rotherhithe | March 1941 |
| TF57 | Odessa Wharf, Rotherhithe | September 1940 |
| TF98 | Lawrence's Wharf, Rotherhithe | 1941 |
| TF68 | Imperial Wharf, Bankside | May 1941 |
| TF78 | Mark Brown's Wharf, Southwark | May 1941 |
| TF88 | Kitchen's Wharf, Bermondsey | May 1941 |
| TF99 | Farmiloe's Wharf, Southwark | March 1942 |
| TF117 | Montreal Wharf, Bermondsey | August 1944 |
| TF118 | Bond's Granary, Bermondsey | August 1944 |

The designated rendezvous point at which the T-F personnel would, when required, meet up with squads of Royal Engineers or a heavy rescue team was in Lower Road, Bermondsey, the south entrance to the Rotherhithe Tunnel; the reinforcements could thus be drafted in from the north or south bank.

## Selected Incidents

### TF21 Trinity & Durand's Wharves, Rotherhithe

These two adjacent wharves lay close to the Surrey Docks and, like them, specialized in handling and storing timber. The 1937 panorama shows timber stacked on the wharfside, in the cavernous sheds behind, on the barges berthed alongside, and lashed together in rafts floating in the river (Ellmers & Werner, 1988, pp. 72–3). On 7-8 September 1940, the first major raid on London, these two wharves were both hit, and a conflagration engulfed them and their stockpiles of timber. The wharf-facing and the flood defences at the head of Laystall Stairs were all built of timber and they too were very badly damaged: a 400ft length of timber facing on Durand's Wharf was destroyed. The general ground level behind the wharf lay 2–3ft lower than the standard level. Emergency repairs entailed raking bomb debris up along the frontage and the securing of the secondary line of flood defences, set further inland. Temporary repair work by No. 695 Company of the Royal Engineers began on 24 October and included the construction of a concrete parapet wall along the entire length of Durand's Wharf: this can be seen in the middle ground, rising above the re-clad timber frontage and returning inland to join up with

T-F incidents nos 21/22, Trinity to Durand's Wharf. The busy river frontage is seen here in 1937, from South Wharf, where the AFS operated a fire-float station, to Lawrence's Dock. Trinity Wharf dealt primarily in timber, often softwoods, seasoned in the sheds behind the quayside upon which recently offloaded planking is stacked. (© *Museum of London: PLA Collection 322708*)

the shell of the burned-out brick building. To the south, Laystall Stairs were defended with a sandbag wall.

Before all these works could be completed (a substantial task that took until 26 November 1940), there was a major alarm on Sunday, 3 November. This was not, however, the Luftwaffe. Indeed, the then Prime Minister Winston

In 1937, timber cargoes were also accommodated at the adjacent Durand's Wharf. (© *Museum of London: PLA Collection 322714*)

A local landmark: this crenellated warehouse was part of Lawrence and Company's Surrey Rice Mills development in 1937. (© *Museum of London: PLA Collection 322712*)

Churchill recalled that 'for the first time in nearly two months no alarm sounded in London. The silence seemed quite odd to many.' The threat was from the rising river, for Scotland Yard informed County Hall that the high tide observed at Southend was already 2ft (0.6m) higher than predicted. This phone call from Southend was a manifestation of the new 'flood early-

Bombed out: the devastation to wharves, warehouses and river wall from Trinity to Durand's Wharf after the bomb strikes in 1940. (© *LMA: TDP, P. Kennedy TF211116*)

warning system' set up in the aftermath of the 1928 disaster. The message was quickly relayed by Mr Simmonds to Mr French at the T-F depot in Southwark. The defences at Durand's Wharf were still under construction at this date and thus could be compromised all too easily by such an exceptionally high tide. Observations on site at 5.00pm recorded no visible overflow, but Simmonds and French, ever mindful of the real danger, dutifully returned to the site at 9.00pm with torches. By then, the river had indeed overtopped the wharf frontage, but the secondary defences seem to have held, with only shallow water lapping Rotherhithe Street itself. The police had already been notified of the potential risks and some local underground shelters had been evacuated. All in all, this was a close shave: the nightmare scenario had been avoided, just.

That the Luftwaffe did not mount a major raid on London that night could be seen as further proof that London's extreme vulnerability to flooding was not a strategic consideration for the Nazi war machine. That said, the foul weather in the Channel – the consequence of the extreme low pressure that raised the river levels – also made the taking-off and landing of large bombers on the north European coast rather more risky than Göring wished. One way or another, London's river defences were not tested that night; had there been a major raid, the city could well have been swamped. The Thames-Flood unit was clearly shaken by this astonishing 'near miss', and wrote a letter on 9 November to the Director of the Met Office at the Air Ministry in Stonehouse, Gloucestershire. They pointed out that much earlier notification of abnormal high tides 'would be of great assistance': the early-warning system was not early enough. Their plea was acknowledged by the 20th of the month.

A year later in September 1941, further work was required on the defences in Rotherhithe, following salvage clearance on the site that disturbed the sandbag walling. No further work was undertaken here until the 'semipermanent' repair programme commenced at the south end of Durand's Wharf and Laystall Stairs, running from 21 January 1943 to 12 March 1943. The last recorded phases of works to the secondary line of defences, necessitated by the deterioration of the sandbags here, was in early 1944, followed in October of that year by further repair work following the demolition of other parts of the secondary defences. Thus it seems that some sandbags were expected to serve for years rather than months.

## TF40 Brandram's and Ginesi

On 29 December 1940, the upstream section of Brandram's four-storey waterfront warehouse was burned out and part of the river wall on the neighbouring wharf owned by S. Ginesi & Co. was demolished. The breach was filled with debris, as was the building itself, and clearance could not begin

T-F incident no. 40, Brandram's Wharf. This 1870s' warehouse was operated by G. Stephenson & Co.; the roofed crane driver's cabin can be seen at first-floor level. The business handled paper and cardboard on the eve of the Blitz, while the adjacent Ginesi Wharf dealt with less flammable marbles. (© *Museum of London: PLA Collection 322736*)

until July the following year. Once cleared, a wall of 600 sandbags was built to secure the river defences. That should have marked the end of this particular phase, but the repair attracted rather more attention than was anticipated and bags went missing. The 'disturbance' was sufficient to merit its rebuilding in concrete bagwork. Unfortunately an inspection in the depths of a cold winter revealed that this had also been 'disturbed', and the T-F team resorted to using ballast-filled bags as concrete would not set 'owing to frost'. A later inspection then found that some concrete bags had even been thrown in the river, presumably by local children, unaware of the importance of the flood defences. The T-F team then rebuilt the wall in concrete in March 1942, a solution that kept both the Thames and London's younger residents in check until the permanent repairs were completed more than four years later in October 1946.

Our recent fieldwork has not only identified part of the 1940s' brick parapet that replaced the bagwork, but actually recorded a concrete bag on the foreshore; it would be interesting to speculate whether or not it was one of those noted with such justifiable irritation by the Thames-Flood inspector in 1941.

The warehouse had been used to store paper and cardboard, contents that would have added fuel to the fire that burned out G.H. Stephenson's building. The wall-mounted crane on the riverside façade was also badly damaged in the raid, and the lookum (the roofed cabin that housed the crane operative) was destroyed. However, it seems that this facility had been rented from the PLA since January 1929, and G.H. Stephenson was still being charged £8 per annum for it the year after the raid, as a letter dated 29 October 1941 in the PLA archive shows. The wharfinger replied to the PLA, politely suggesting that the demand should be adjusted accordingly as the crane had not been used since December 1940. Leaving nothing to chance, the PLA then inspected the site and confirmed that the lookum had indeed gone, but noted that 'the crane still exists', although admittedly 'in a damaged condition'. The matter could be resolved, however. The deputy river superintendent suggested that 'Removal of the crane will enable me to cancel the licence and the rent will cease on day of completion.'

Saving face. Brandram's Wharf warehouse in 2010, showing that the eastern half of the façade (right), which had been blown out during the Blitz, has now been restored but with square-headed windows on the first three floors. (© *TDP, TF40*)

Waterfront parapet abutting Brandram's warehouse and extending onto Ginesi's Wharf also shows evidence of repairs after bomb damage. (© *TDP*, *TF40*)

Although the crane may have survived in some form, it seems unlikely that the warehouse or wharf could have been operative in 1941. Correspondence in February 1942 shows that G.H. Stephenson wished to engage Messrs John Shelbourne & Co. to clear debris on the foreshore 'consisting of brickwork, cement and steel pieces, up to 6ft high in places' covering an area of 80ft by 50ft in front of the wharf. The cost of such clearance was estimated at £182.10s, a sum that the wharfinger hoped he could set against a claim to the Board of Trade under the War Damage Act. A letter dated 13 February 1942 from the PLA suggested some support, suggesting that 'the removal of the debris will restore to the wharf its former facilities for the berthing of craft.'

The plight of the wharfinger was still not over, however. Just two years later, in 1944, a flying bomb exploded on the foreshore at Brandram's Wharf, damaging the surrounding properties, including the recently-repaired warehouse. It also completely destroyed the campsheeting of the barge bed: the destruction was such that the engineer called in to reinstate the site in 1951

A 1940s' sandbag? During the Thames Discovery Programme's survey of the blitzed building debris on the modern foreshore at Brandram's, an example of concrete bagwork was found, perhaps a survival from 1940s' repair works. (© *TDP*)

(from Messrs John Shelbourne & Co.) doubted that there had ever been any campsheeting there at all. G.H. Stephenson insisted emphatically that there had been, and supplied a plan of 1938 'shewing campsheeting marked "existing"'. The point at issue here was that the PLA would not levy any extra charge for reinstatement, but would demand a fee of *c.* £5 per annum if it was a new work. The issue was resolved by letter on 5 December 1951, some six years after the rocket strike.

Another letter in the PLA archives records that refurbishment of the parapet at R.T. Clements' waterfront property at Ginesi Wharf (adjoining the western side of Brandram's Wharf) was to commence in July 1947. This was to be conducted with a licence from the Ministry of Works 'to carry out certain War Damage repairs.' That work required a tubular scaffold to be erected on the foreshore, some 30ft long and extending 4ft from the old river wall. The 'existing temporary dam' was to be taken down and the flood wall rebuilt. Whether the works being replaced were the initial response to the strikes in 1940 or 1944 is not recorded, but do show that waterfront reinstatement was often a protracted affair and that the adjective 'temporary' when used for flood defences could indeed refer to years rather than months.

The dates on this correspondence also show that it took time to rebuild and refurbish the Thames-side warehouses and wharves: VE Day marked the end of hostilities, but getting the waterfront back to full working order would take a little longer. Indeed, for many of the private river-based wharves that had been badly damaged, the sites never returned to commercial use.

### TF41 Yardley's Wharf

These nineteenth-century granaries were destroyed in December 1940, and the front wall of the warehouse, which formed the river wall, was completely demolished down to 4ft (1.3m) below the 'safe' standard level. However, the quantity of debris that covered the site prevented close inspection, but a temporary sandbag wall was built across the breach on 17 January 1941. Further works were required in April, but once the debris had been cleared, it was observed that the warehouse had a 6ft-deep basement on the riverside, which was considered unstable. Further works were required in October 1941, which saw the river wall raised to the required standard. It is suggested that

T-F incident no. 41, Yardley's Wharf. View of the Thames waterfront looking downstream towards Yardley's Wharf in 2010. (© *TDP*)

Shuttered concrete river wall repair below Yardley's Wharf, photographed in 2018. (© *TDP, A. Broomfield*)

the shuttered concrete waterfront wall still visible today from the foreshore represents the latter stages of this repair programme.

## TF68 Imperial Wharf

This site in Bankside was one of many hit during the raid on 10 May 1941, destroying a crane, 40ft of the river wall down to the foreshore, and damaging the parapet on either side of the crater. During the night, a wall containing

T-F incident no. 68, Imperial Wharf, Bankside. The top of the new sandbag defence can just be seen on the landward edge of the crater, together with the team who worked through the night to build it. (© *LMA: TDP, P. Kennedy TF68*)

2,000 sandbags was begun around the landward edge of the crater and, after daylight, this was extended on both sides up to the surviving wall. The top of the sandbag defence can just be seen, as can the team who worked through the night to build it, just to the right of the surviving crane. The permanent reinstatement began on 18 June 1941, with the construction of a cofferdam, within which the new river wall was constructed. This was completed on 4 February 1942, some eight months later.

All trace of this has disappeared under modern redevelopment. Even the warehouses that survived the Blitz have been replaced, in this instance by a timber-framed thatched building that would not have survived an incendiary attack.

### TF78 Mark Brown's Wharf
The waterfront warehouses were hit by HEs, badly damaging the façade and river frontage during the infamous raid on 10 May 1941. Some 80ft of river wall was demolished well below the standard level. The temporary repairs took some time, with the initial wall of 960 sandbags not completed until August 1941, with further moveable dams being set further back in November of that year. The permanent repairs were more substantial and took six months to finish, with work continuing from 30 September 1942 to 29 March 1943, clearly representing a major programme of works.

T-F incident no. 78, Mark Brown's Wharf. This large warehouse, built in 1914, was part of a busy wharf that handled a variety of canned goods and general cargo in 1937.
(© *Museum of London: PLA Collection 322776*)

Supporting the GLA. Although hard to see under the aquatic growths, this modern view of the waterfront wall on the site of Mark Brown's Wharf has one section built in brick (to the left of the drain outlet) but with shuttered concrete beyond. The latter is probably the repair to the bomb strike in 1941 designed by LCC's T-F team. Some eighty years later, it protects City Hall, the HQ of the Greater London Authority, the successor body to LCC. (*TDP, TF78*)

### TF117/118 Montreal Wharf/Bond's Granary

These two riverside granaries are shown in full working order in the 1937 panorama, with the spillage from the sacks of flour evident on the building's façade (and on the warehousemen inside). The buildings suffered a direct hit from a rocket on 4 August 1944, but the breach to the river wall was blocked by debris and also by a huge mound of flour, described by the T-F inspector as 'a dumpling'. The site could not be worked on until the building debris had

T-F incidents nos 117/118, Bond's Wharf. The white staining on the façade of the nineteenth-century granaries show that Henry Bellingham's firm was handling flour in 1937. (© *Museum of London: PLA Collection 322755*)

Chamber's Wharf: this complex, next to Bond's Wharf, was expanding and rebuilding in 1937, developing a business that handled a variety of foodstuffs. (© *Museum of London: PLA Collection 322762*)

Fire-fighters tackle the blaze in the Chamber's Wharf warehouses in 1944.
(*Mary Evans Picture Library: © London Fire Brigade 10534890*)

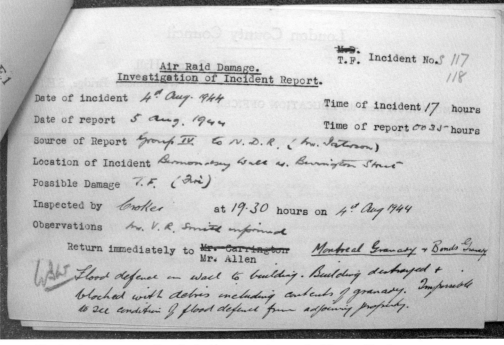

been cleared, which had been done by December 1944. A wall of concrete bagwork was then constructed by a team of two or three men in ten days. The more permanent repair programme took two months, but was not completed until November 1946, nearly two years later, when the war was well and truly over.

Recent fieldwork noted that although most of the site has now been cleared, following the demolition of the Chamber's Wharf complex, a small section of the 1940s' river wall, with a shuttered concrete parapet, was still visible immediately east of the projecting jetty. The rest was encased behind steel sheet piling erected during the redevelopment of the wharf in the 1960s, and subsequently by the work on the Combined Sewage Overflow for the Thames super sewer, built in the twenty-first century.

*Chapter Six*

# Stoneyard: The Battersea Depot

The location of the T-F depot in Battersea Park is the best-preserved of the four Thames-Flood centres, set in the walled compound of the Stoneyard, now the home of the Park Police. During the war, the Thames-Flood team shared the rest of the park with the temporary tents of various military units, an anti-aircraft emplacement, some 7,000 allotments and a pig farm, as Londoners dug for victory. The region in which the depot operated spanned both banks of the Thames, as they would respond to incidents in Wandsworth and Lambeth as often as in Fulham and Westminster. The park was thus well placed, since it had the Albert Bridge to one side and Chelsea Bridge on the other, while a third 'Emergency Bridge' was built running directly from the depot to the Chelsea Embankment. The designated rendezvous point, at which the T-F personnel would, when required, meet up with squads of Royal Engineers or a heavy rescue team, was at Vauxhall Cross, at the junction of Vauxhall Bridge approach. This lay a little further to the east, allowing ready access to Lambeth and Pimlico, both vulnerable, low-lying areas.

One of the incidents to which the team responded was very close to home, on the river wall in Battersea Park itself. A 45ft section of the parapet wall was destroyed, requiring a temporary repair of 750 sandbags. A more permanent reinstatement was undertaken in March 1941, using labour drawn from the Bridges Division, the team building the emergency bridge at the other end of the Park.

## Selected Incidents

### TF05 Embankment, Westminster

The first night of the Blitz saw an HE bomb explode on the foreshore near HMS *President*, and the blast demolished 50ft (7m) of the Victoria Embankment's parapet down to footway level. Joints in the granite facing were opened up over a distance of 170ft, and part of the wall was tilted forwards. The river police, who were kept very busy that night and were not fully *au fait* with the T-F unit's organization and procedures, reported the incident to the Pyrimont Wharf depot. The information had thus to be relayed to Battersea, from whence a team finally set out to repair the damage. By 14 September, all the parapet stones bar one had been temporarily replaced and backed up with 500 sandbags, while the gap was filled with a timber and clay dam.

View across Battersea Bridge to the fire station. (© *LMA 211744*)

However, it was not just the parapet wall that had suffered: below the pavement, the brickwork forming the arch of the subway now had a crack 170ft long, while the gas mains were fractured and the electrical cables displaced. Nothing could be done here until the parapet had been secured, and so

| | **Incidents Attended by the Battersea Team** | |
|---|---|---|
| TF04 | Southern Railway, Nine Elms, Lambeth | September 1940 |
| TF05 | Victoria Embankment, Westminster | September 1940 |
| TF10 | National Wharf, Fulham | September 1940 |
| TF11 | Craven Cottage, Fulham | September 1940 |
| TF13 | Aird's & Darfield's Wharf, Lambeth | October 1940) |
| TF13a | Kings Arm's Wharf, Lambeth | October 1940 |
| TF16 | Bishop's Park, Fulham | October 1940 |
| TF17 | Princes Wharf, Wandsworth | October 1940 |
| TF19 | India Store Depot, Lambeth | October 1940 |
| TF24 | Ram Brewery, Wandsworth | November 1940 |
| TF27 | Prescott Wharf, Wandsworth | November 1940 |
| TF28 | Providence Sufferance Wharf, Lambeth | October 1940 |
| TF28a | Providence Sufferance Wharf, Lambeth | May 1941 |
| TF29 | Battersea Park, Wandsworth | November 1940 |
| TF33 | Imperial Wharf, Westminster | December 1940 |
| TF33a | Cambridge Wharf, Westminster | December 1940 |
| TF58 | Meux Brewery, Wandsworth | April 1941 |
| TF59 | Dolphin Square, Pimlico | April 1941 |
| TF60 | Victoria Gardens, Westminster | April 1941 |
| TF61 | Lacks Draw Dock, Lambeth | April 1941 |
| TF62 | Parliament Wharf, Westminster | April 1941 |
| TF63 | Albert Embankment, Lambeth | April 1941 |
| TF28a | Providence Sufferance Wharf, Lambeth | May 1941 |
| TF70 | Anderson's Garage, Westminster | May 1941 |
| TF71 | Phillips Mills, Wandsworth | May 1941 |
| TF72 | Watson House, Wandsworth | May 1941 |
| TF73 | Portland Wharf, Westminster | May 1941 |
| TF92 | Moore's Transport, Lambeth | September 1941 |
| TF102 | Wandsworth Wharf, Wandsworth | February 1944 |
| TF106 | Belmont Works: Price, Battersea | July 1944 |
| TF107 | Sherwood Wharf, Battersea | July 1944 |
| TF108 | Victoria Embankment | July 1944 |
| TF109 | Belmont Works, Battersea | July 1944 |
| TF110 | Southampton Wharf, Battersea | July 1944 |
| TF112 | Cleopatra's Needle, Westminster | July 1944 |
| TF113 | Belgrave Dock, Westminster | July 1944) |

permanent reinstatement of this section quickly began and was completed by 5 October. The sandbags were no longer required and were thus made ready for re-use elsewhere, and attention could turn to replacing the arched roof of the subway.

## TF11 Craven Cottage

Some 50ft of the river wall at the very north end of the site was demolished in September 1940, and a sandbag wall was built around the edge of the crater to secure the site temporarily. Three months later, the impoverished owners of this site, Fulham Football Club, intimated that they could not afford to pay for permanent repairs. Discussions then ensued about how more robust works

T-F incident no. 11, Craven Cottage. Bomb damage to the river wall at the upstream end of Fulham Football Club's ground, next to an industrial wharf. (*Below*) Extensive scouring of ground made unstable exposed by the bomb. (© *LMA: TDP, P. Kennedy TF111071 & 1072*)

The 1940s' shuttered concrete repair at Craven Cottage, looking somewhat the worse for wear some eighty years later. (*TDP, TF11*)

The location of the bomb strike (to the left) in relation to the Fulham Football Stadium in 2010. (*TDP, TF11*)

could be implemented, while the damaged site deteriorated. The Port of London Authority complained of shoals and scour on the site in July 1941, ten months after the initial strike. A solution had to be found, given Fulham FC's continuing poverty, and so a semi-permanent repair was instigated by Unit Construction in six weeks, paid for under the Housing Contract. The result, a shuttered concrete wall grafted onto the remnants of the earlier brickwork, was still visible in 2010, although looking rather the worse for wear. Hopefully the club's finances have improved sufficiently over the intervening seventy years to allow them, if required, to remedy the situation without recourse to outside help.

### TF13 Darfield Waste Paper Company
The north-east corner of the Darfield's Wharf and 45ft of the river wall on the adjacent Aird's Wharf were destroyed on 8 October 1940. The ground level behind the wharf was between +15ft and +16ft above OD, whereas the standard level for flood defences here was required to be +19ft OD. Starting in daylight on 9 October, a wall of 3,750 sandbags was constructed around the perimeter of the breach, a task that took 700 man hours over ten days. The breach itself was filled with bomb debris to prevent further scour.

The site owners had just begun repairing the damaged walls of the adjacent warehouse when it was destroyed by fire in another raid in February 1941. It

T-F incident no. 13, Aird's and Darfield's. The site of this major breach of the river defences, in the shadow of the Shot Tower in 1940, now lies under the Royal Festival Hall. (© *LMA: TDP, P. Kennedy TF131081*)

was subsequently decided to undertake semi-permanent repairs to the river wall to stabilize the situation, using concrete bagwork laid sloping upwards from just above the foreshore level, finishing in a 3ft-high parapet, also in concrete bagwork. Starting in September 1941, this took two months and 4,000 bags at a cost of £1,022.9s.1d.

Further support for the parapet was provided by concrete in one section, and with rubble and sandbags in another. The same treatment was given to the top of the river wall at the adjacent King's Arms Wharf, when the robust demolition of the burned-out buildings by the WDS lowered the river wall there below the standard level in November 1941.

These wharves lay in the shadow of the Shot Tower, a famous Lambeth landmark; this survived the war and was a feature of the Festival of Britain site in the brave new world of 1951. For that event, a large area of the waterfront was comprehensively redeveloped: Darfield's Wastepaper Co. and the repairs to the riverfront described above were subsumed under the South Bank's brand-new Royal Festival Hall complex. Once the festival was over, even the Shot Tower, along with the much-lamented Skylon, disappeared from the London skyline, just as the T-F's handiwork has disappeared from the riverfront.

## TF16 Bishop's Park, Fulham
On 16 October 1940, following damage by enemy action, 100ft (30m) of the river wall collapsed onto the foreshore. The ground behind was very loose, and the threat of river scour opening up the crater was considerable. Sandbags were thus piled around the crater's edge to counteract the threat of further

erosion. Semi-permanent works then commenced using pitched tiers of concrete bagwork secured behind a small wall set on the foreshore. This work needed 5,000 bags and took three months to complete. According to the T-F log book, a decision on a more permanent solution was 'suspended' (for the duration of the war), and thus the bagwork served as the river wall here for at least another four or five years.

The correspondence files reveal another aspect of this incident. The pile of debris on the foreshore, comprising large angular stone blocks from the initial blast, was seen as a navigation hazard, one of many on the Thames during the Blitz. As such, it had to be marked with a wreck skiff to prevent damage to any of the many boats and barges then using the river. The skiff remained moored there until the masonry was cleared, some two and a half months later. While it was agreed that the temporary repairs were paid for by LCC, the cost incurred by the hire of the skiff from the PLA – some £22.10s – was a matter of some debate. According to a letter dated 31 May 1941, neither LCC nor the borough of Fulham thought it their responsibility and therefore were not prepared to pay. It is positively heartening to see that budgets were being scrutinized so carefully at a time when London's rebuilding costs were near incalculable, especially following the raid of 10 May just three weeks earlier.

The T-F log book does not record when the permanent repairs were undertaken, but study of the site suggests it was clearly a no-expense-spared peacetime initiative, in which the masonry blocks have been carefully replaced to produce a seamless façade at river level. The only indicators of the area of repair are the form of the drainage outlets which, unlike the originals, are not

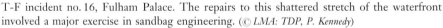

T-F incident no.16, Fulham Palace. The repairs to this shattered stretch of the waterfront involved a major exercise in sandbag engineering. (© *LMA: TDP, P. Kennedy*)

Young archaeologists provide the human scales for the now-repaired section of the Fulham waterfront in 2010. (*TDP, N. Cohen*)

countersunk, and the number of coats of paint on the replacement iron balustrade, rather fewer on the repaired section than on the Victorian work.

### TF59 Dolphin Square

On 16 April 1941 an HE bomb exploded just behind the river wall in front of Dolphin Square, destroying 70ft of the brick river wall and leaving a crater 15ft deep and 70ft across. As an emergency measure, debris was piled up around the edge of the crater, and this was augmented by some 250 sandbags at the downstream end of the site. (It is thought that this wharf was being used for the storage of coal at the time, revetted piles of which can be seen in the middle ground in the contemporary photograph. Some of this precious commodity apparently spilled out onto the foreshore, and a houseboat owner who lived here in the post-war period claimed he was able to collect his fuel from there for many years.)

In 1941 the T-F team approached the site owners to repair the river wall. A copy of the Planning Regulations TF/ARP/9/1941 was sent to Dolphin Square Ltd, suggesting the form of works which the T-F team deemed suitable, and subsequently plans were agreed for the reinstatement. The repairs were carried out over three months, completing on 3 November 1941. Study of the shuttered concrete and brickwork façade that now fills the breach site suggests not one but two phases of repair work to this river wall.

T-F incident no. 59, Dolphin Square; river wall breached in residential Pimlico. (© *LMA: TDP, P. Kennedy*)

Bomb damage at Dolphin Square repaired, partially in brick, partially in shuttered concrete, as recorded in 2010. (*TDP, P. Kennedy TF59*)

## TF60 Victoria Tower Embankment Gardens

The raid on the night of 16/17 April 1941 was particularly severe, involving 890 tons of high explosives and 100,000 incendiaries, causing 8 major fires, 41 serious incidents and more than 2,000 'smaller' ones. There was widespread damage across London, including hits on the Houses of Parliament, while in the gardens adjoining the Victoria Tower, the River Police reported a serious bomb strike on the morning of 17 April; there was a breach in the river wall over 20ft across reaching almost down to the foreshore. The parapet and coping stones either side of the crater were also damaged and a debris field was still visible on the foreshore seventy-five years later. Judging by the size of the crater, it has been suggested that it was caused by an SC50 (*Sprengbombe Cylindrisch* 50kg), a standard air-dropped munition used by the Luftwaffe (Chris Kolonko pers. comm.).

The ground level behind the wall was more than 3ft below the standard level, and the site lies ominously close to the location where the great flood of 1928 inundated a large area. A temporary debris dam was therefore rapidly piled up around the external perimeter of the crater, after which the Battersea team filled 2,500 sandbags at their depot (this task alone took 144 man hours), which were then transported to the site. Here, a five-man team seconded from the Borough of Westminster took nine days to build the sandbag defence 3ft 6in high and 3ft wide at the base all the way round the crater's edge. This secured the site until the government's own Office of Works began the reinstatement, working from 15 May to 1 August.

T-F incident no. 60, Victoria Tower Gardens. The Embankment next to the Houses of Parliament was seriously breached, as shown in this 1941 photograph.
(© *LMA: TDP, P. Kennedy TF601268*)

TF60: filled-in river wall breach of the Embankment wall, next to the Houses of Parliament, the intended target. A major flood here could have done even more damage. (*TDP, P. Kennedy*)

The result can still be seen today: the breach has been filled with concrete, here scored to imitate the ashlar granite courses of the rest of the embankment walling in an attempt to disguise the patch. A similar ruse has been noted in Sheffield by Chris Kolonko: the Wicker Arches were struck by a bomb that penetrated them but failed to explode. The hole was repaired with shuttered concrete and, as on the London Embankment, it was incised with lines reflecting the original stone courses.

As for the parapet, this has also been rebuilt in concrete, now rather weathered, and further strengthened with a large concrete buttress on the landward side. The rough-and-ready workmanship shown here in the shadow of the Houses of Parliament is as good an indication of the austerity of those desperate times as any: there was no time for carefully-cut masonry, and no attempt to disguise the buttress. The surprise is surely that these repairs are still here, seventy years on.

Of all the surviving examples of 1940s' river wall repair, this location is arguably the most accessible and most obvious, the scar even being visible from the Albert Embankment on the opposite side of the river when the tide is out. Consequently this was the site selected for the plaque installed in 2014 to commemorate the work of Peirson Frank and his Thames-Flood team.

According to the entry in the log book, the strike is recorded as happening on 16 March, while the event was noted as being reported on 17 April. The

TF60: shuttered concrete repair of the Victoria Tower Gardens breach; note scored lines replicating the adjacent coursed masonry. (*TDP, P. Kennedy*)

TF60: the survey team records the blast debris spread on the Westminster foreshore (centre) and the filled-in breach in the river wall (right). (*TDP, N. Cohen*)

TF60: debris from the river wall blown up in 1941 still lying on the modern foreshore. (*TDP, P. Kennedy*)

TF60: concrete repair plinth on the internal face of the Embankment parapet, seventy-five years later. (*TDP*)

first date is clearly a transcription error: 16/17 March was a quiet night for London, while the night of 16/17 April was quite the reverse.

### TF71 Phillips, Mills & Co.

One of the many incidents recorded in the T-F log book for the dreadful raid on 10 May 1941 concerns this waste paper merchant's wharf next to Battersea Bridge. A bomb had exploded on the foreshore, exposing the foundations of the river wall for a length of 30ft and a depth of 3ft, the blast also damaging the parapet. The rest of the entry summarily states that the T-F team was not required to undertake any temporary works, since the owners themselves carried out the necessary repairs to the foundation. No dates or costs are appended in the log book entry.

Further illumination has, however, been found by Sally Mashiter in the Port of London Authority (PLA) archives, with the surviving contemporary (1941) correspondence between the PLA, Phillips, Mills & Co. and a civil engineering contractor, John Shelbourne & Co. Study of these letters shows that this particular incident was resolved by 10 June, i.e. exactly one month after the bomb strike. Nevertheless, it can be deduced that, since the bomb clearly produced a considerable pile of debris, the incident was rather more damaging than the deceptively curt note in the T-F log book suggests. The eleven documents are transcribed below.

The matter-of-fact content of the letters – drafted by the official and then typed by a secretary in the pre-email era – provides yet another example of the 'keep calm and carry on' approach to the challenges faced by London after

**71.**

INCIDENT  Phillips Mills, Battersea
Wandsworth. 746 B - 749.

DATE  10th May 1941      REPORTED  BY

DESCRIPTION
Bomb on foreshore. Ground blown out from foundation of river wall for length of about 30 ft and to a depth back under of about 3 ft. Slight damage to rear top of wall

TEMPORARY  REPAIRS
Commenced              Completed
          None required

PERMANENT  REPAIRS
          Owners carried out repair to foundation

T-F incident no. 71, Phillips Mills & Co. Reading between the lines: compare the protracted correspondence concerning this major incident with this terse account in the T-F log book. (© *LMA: TDP, P. Kennedy*)

each and every raid. Even more significantly, the correspondence also demonstrates that it was not just LCC's Thames-Flood team that continued to take a concerned interest in bomb-damaged waterfront sites, badgering the owners of the blitzed site to effect a sound repair. The PLA were equally persistent in their demands, and the rather terse tone is set with the first of the letters from the Harbour Master. London was still trying to operate as a working port, regardless of the Luftwaffe's attentions. Navigation along the river and berthing at the upriver wharves was beset by wrecks and bomb debris, which when covered at high tide could prove a danger to barges and other shipping. It was the Harbour Master's job to ensure that green flags on buoys marked all such potential obstructions.

(1) PLA Harbour Master to Phillips, Mills & Co., 19 May 1941:

> Dear Sirs,
> Re debris and wreckage on foreshore and riverside berths I am informed that as a result of enemy action, debris and wreckage from your premises at Bridge Wharf, Battersea has fallen onto the foreshore. It is of paramount importance in the general interest of the port that berths alongside the river wharves be kept clear of wreckage and although your difficulties at the present time are fully appreciated, I have to remind you of your responsibility to put in hand the work of removal as soon as possible. I shall be glad of your assurance that clearance work will be undertaken at an early date. In the meantime the debris should be marked as an obstruction to navigation: please let me know if you will arrange for this to be done.
> Yours Faithfully
> Harbour Master

(2) The reply from Phillips, Mills & Co. to PLA River Superintendent, London EC3 (no more detailed address was required) is on headed notepaper, dated 21 May 1941. The Post Office was operating efficiently, since the letter was stamped as having arrived the very next day, on 22 May. As regards obstructions, the implication here is that the damage was considerable, since several tidal windows would still be required to remove the debris, ten days after the raid.

> Dear Sir,
> We beg to inform you that arrangements have been made for the removal of the foreshore obstruction on the next tide, and we anticipate being able to remove all the material within the next two tides.
> Yours Faithfully,
> General Manager

(3) The General Manager seems to have been rather over-optimistic in his appraisal of the damage, and the true state of the site becomes more apparent in this reply from the PLA, dated 26 May 1941, sent to Phillips, Mills & Co.:

Dear Sirs,
Further to my letter of the 19th instant (letter no. 1 above), further collapse of debris on to the foreshore at Bridge Wharf Battersea has made it imperative that marking be carried out without delay, and that the Harbour Service has placed a green flag at the site. Charges are payable for the service, and an account will be rendered to you in due course,
Yours Faithfully,
Deputy River Superintendent

(4) Phillips, Mills & Co.'s reply to the PLA was dated 27 May 1941 (once again demonstrating that the Royal Mail was operating an efficient next-day delivery service). This letter shows signs of irritation, perhaps justified for a company that has had its wharf and livelihood badly damaged:

Dear Sir
We have your letter of 26 May and we assume you have already received our reply to yours of the 19th, in which we indicated that all debris lying on the foreshore at Bridge Wharf, Battersea, was being removed on the day we wrote to you. This was carried out and we presume so far as we are concerned that the green flag placed on the site can now be removed. May we draw attention to the fact that there is still a very large bomb hole on the foreshore confronting this wharf and maybe at your earliest convenience you will be attending to this.
Yours Faithfully
General Manager

(5) The PLA wasted no time in replying with the next letter of 28 May 1941. Their ever-watchful team had already inspected the site and, once again, the damage sounds severe and the condition of the wharf unstable. As for the filling in of the bomb crater, their response is noteworthy, not least because the complainant had just removed a vast amount of debris from the site:

Dear Sir,
Debris of the Foreshore
In reply to your letter of the 27th inst, I understand that since you cleared the first quantity of debris from the foreshore at Bridge Wharf Battersea, part of the wharf crane with some debris has collapsed on to the foreshore. The marking is necessary because of the crane wreckage.

With regard to the bomb crater on the berth of the wharf, the filling of this is thought to be primarily a matter for yourselves, as frontagers, as you doubtless intend to invite craft to the berth in the course of your use of the wharf.

In the circumstances, permission is hereby given to you to fill in the hole with rubble and to level with a top dressing of chalk, provided there is no interference with the berths of your neighbours and that the work is carried out to the authority's satisfaction.

Yours Faithfully,

Deputy River Superintendent

(6) Phillips, Mills & Co. do not seem to have replied immediately to the PLA on that score, since they were also discussing wharf repair plans with LCC's T-F unit and with a contractor, Shelbournes, who might undertake this urgent work. It was the latter who now wrote to the PLA. Interestingly, both organizations shared the same address – Port of London Building, Trinity Square EC3. John Shelbourne & Co. Ltd wrote to PLA River Superintendent 30 May 1941:

Dear Sirs,

Messrs Phillips, Mills & Co. Ltd have sustained damage by a bomb at their Battersea Wharf, the river wall being undermined. In consultation with the Floods Prevention Dept, LCC, we have formulated a proposal for the repairs as shown in the enclosed drawing, but before taking the matter any further we should be glad to know whether such a scheme would have your sanction,

Yours Faithfully

John Shelbourne & Co.

(7) Having rapidly reviewed the plans submitted, the PLA's standard response letter to Shelbourne & Co. is dated 31 May 1941:

Referring to your letter of the 30th instant, permission is hereby given to effect repairs to the river wall at Phillips, Mills & Co.'s wharf at Battersea in accordance with your plan No. 3760, provided that the work is carried out to the Authority's satisfaction. If any variation is found necessary in the scheme of reconstruction, kindly notify me before completion.

Yours Faithfully,

Deputy River Superintendent

(8) Shelbourne & Co. replied to the PLA on 3 June, but we have no record of when or how the river wall was actually repaired. Photographs taken in 1982

suggest the upper levels were rebuilt in brick, but the base might have been strengthened with shuttered concrete behind a temporary coffer dam:

> Dear Sir
> We acknowledge the receipt of your letter of the 31st ult, favouring us sanction to proceed with the repairs to above wharf, for which we thank you. Should any variation in the scheme of reconstruction be found necessary we will at once communicate with you on the matter.
> Yours Faithfully
> John Shelbourne & Co.

(9) Phillips, Mills & Co. finally wrote to the PLA on 7 June 1941, stating that the site had now been cleared, although it is not clear whether or not the river wall repair works had commenced:

> Dear Sir,
> We refer to your letter of 28 May in which you mention the debris on the foreshore of Bridge Wharf. We are pleased to advise you that the overhanging debris has now been removed and we presume you will now arrange for the removal of the marking flag.
> Yours Faithfully,
> General Manager

(10) The PLA's Harbour Service team promptly visited the site once again and sent a hand-written confirmation note to Head Office on 10 June 1941:

> Debris on foreshore and collapsed crane etc: I can now confirm that the overhanging crane and other debris has now been cleared away by their people. The filling in of the crater has commenced. We have today collected our green flag which we had marked the obstruction with.

(11) That particular correspondence chain seems to end there, but the 1940s' repairs survived forty years, being replaced in 1982, as this letter to the PLA shows. The letter is dated the 16th, but is date-stamped as arriving at the PLA on the 24th. It seems that the Royal Mail moved much faster during the Blitz:

> From: Bernard Sunley & Sons Ltd civil engineering contractors
> Date: 16 June 1982
> Re: Battersea House Wharf, Battersea Bridge Road, London SW18
> We have been awarded the above noted contract and for your information and records we would advise that works are scheduled to commence on 21 June 1982.
> Yours Faithfully
> Building Manager

# Chapter Seven

# Tunnel Avenue:
# The Greenwich Depot

The T-F team at Greenwich was based near the entrance to the Blackwall Tunnel, north of Church Way, next to a council depot and close to Morden's Wharf. The site seems to have been comprehensively redeveloped since the war, so is hard to locate today. The rendezvous point at which the T-F personnel met up with squads of Royal Engineers or a heavy rescue team was outside St Alphage Church Greenwich, at the junction of Church Street and Nelson Street, from which the squads could move off to Woolwich (with its huge Arsenal complex, a prime target) in one direction, or Deptford in the other. However, on 8 September, Deptford Creek Bridge was struck by an HE bomb, seriously disrupting road traffic to and from Greenwich. Luckily

The T-F's Greenwich depot was next to Enderby Wharf, where this fire-boat is moored. (*Mary Evans Picture Library:* © *London Fire Brigade 10534510*)

| Incidents Attended in the Greenwich Area | | |
|---|---|---|
| TF03 | Siemens Works, Woolwich | September 1940 |
| TF08 | Deptford Power Station, Greenwich | September 1940 |
| TF12 | Thanet Wharf, Deptford Creek, Greenwich | September 1940 |
| TF15 | Morden Wharf, Greenwich | October 1940 |
| TF20 | Royal Arsenal Co-op, Woolwich | October 1940 |
| TF22 | Ordnance Wharf, Greenwich | October 1940 |
| TF25a | Commercial Dock, Pier Wharf, Greenwich | September 1940 |
| TF35 | Hills Wharf, Deptford Creek, Greenwich | 1940 |
| TF36 | Badock's Wharf, Greenwich | December 1940 |
| TF42 | Seager's Yard, Greenwich | April 1941 |
| TF64 | Deptford Wharf, Greenwich | May 1941 |
| TF69 | Molassine Works | May 1941 |
| TF93 | Stoneyard, Deptford Creek, Greenwich | September 1941 |
| TF97 | Talbot's Wharf, Greenwich | October 1941 |
| TF100 | Ship Hotel, Greenwich | December 1942 |
| TF101 | Royal Victoria Yard Deptford, Greenwich | January 1943 |
| TF104 | Caledonia Wharf, Greenwich | June 1944 |
| TF111 | Convoy's Wharf, Deptford | July 1944 |
| TF114 | Tunnel Refineries | July 1944 |
| TF115 | Hollick's Wharf | July 1944 |
| TF116 | Hay Wharf Road, Greenwich | August 1944 |
| TF119 | Stowage, Deptford | March 1945 |

the damage was confined to the eastern approach span. Repairs were soon in hand, with the northern carriageway opened two months later, tramlines were re-laid by the end of November, and traffic was flowing in both directions by 14 December.

The area in which the T-F team operated contained much low-lying ground, and had a huge concentration of industrial complexes, all of which would burn well. The depot was thus kept busy during the first phase of the Blitz, as the list below shows. As with the other depots, work began with a vengeance on 7 September 1940, and continued with several major incidents in 1941. These included a strike at the neighbouring Morden's Wharf (TF15) on 10 October 1940 that demolished the warehouse and the flood defences; 500 sandbags were required to secure the site.

In relative terms, things were quiet in the aftermath of the raid of 10 May. In October 1941 the yard was temporarily closed, although the facilities were retained with the proviso that it would 'reopen if required by further enemy action'. In the event, its workload for the last years of the war was shared between the Southwark Park and Pyrimont Wharf teams. The store huts and office accommodation were then disposed of by the Unit Construction

Company for £90, who removed the structures for re-use 'in connection with post-war housing'. This says something about the structural attributes of the buildings – presumably Nissen hut or similar – and something about the dire need for accommodation after the devastation of the Blitz.

## Selected Incidents

### Greenwich Foot Tunnel

Although not directly the responsibility of the Thames-Flood team, damage to tunnels and bridges also had to be repaired by LCC's Chief Engineer. One such example is given here, to provide an engineering perspective on the T-F's programme. At 5.30pm on 7 September 1940 an HE bomb exploded on the foreshore 12 yards from the river wall, directly over the line of the tunnel. The tile and concrete lining of the tunnel collapsed over a length of 30ft (10m). The Poplar shaft also took a direct hit from an oil-incendiary bomb, destroying the electrics for the lift mechanism, and the Greenwich shaft was hit by another incendiary on the following Sunday.

On 8 September 1940, as the tunnel began filling with water, emergency measures were taken to prevent further collapse: LCC's Chief Engineer visited the site personally to assess the dire situation and initially assessed the damage at £30,000. By 14 September, the entire tunnel was flooded, as were both shafts; it was thought it might take up to three months to pump it all out. However, once the pumps had been installed, it actually took only ten days of continuous pumping to clear sufficient water to provide safe access and start

Greenwich Foot Tunnel. Opened in 1901, this tunnel allowed workers from Greenwich to get to the docks and factories on the opposite shore; the glass dome of the Island Gardens end of the tunnel can be seen to the right of the working wharves. (© *Museum of London: PLA Collection 322072*)

Mending the roof: iron collar inserted into the foot tunnel in 1940 to plug the breach caused by bombing in the Blitz. (*TDP*)

clearing the debris. Since the floor of the tunnel slopes downwards as it approaches the middle of the river, it proved possible to work on the higher end of the tunnel, close to the Poplar shaft, even if the longer, lower section of the tunnel remained partially under water. The initial emergency repairs comprised temporary shuttering, erected from 7 October, to contain the severe leakage. After that, in November and December, a series of some thirty iron collars, each some 21in wide, were bolted into position, unit by unit. This formed a 'mini-tunnel' *c.* 8ft in diameter within the larger tunnel. As the subterranean repairs progressed, watermen started running a private ferry service across the river, for which LCC provided the petrol for the boats until the tunnel reopened.

On 19 March 1941, another HE bomb exploding in the river cracked 60m of tiling in the crown of the tunnel. This was not as damaging as the previous strike, however, and the tunnel was patched up and reopened the following day. Nevertheless, it was decided that no attempt should be made on any more permanent repairs until after the war. Yet some seventy years later, the iron-collared 'temporary works' are still in place, still marking the location of that HE bomb-strike on Black Saturday, 1940.

Detail of segments of the custom-built collar, bolted together in 1940, still functioning in the Foot Tunnel eighty years later. (*TDP*)

### TF03 Siemens Works

Another casualty in the first day of the Blitz was the river wall near Siemens factory: the concrete parapet was destroyed, initially only for a length of some 15ft. However, this was followed a fortnight later by a much more serious breach that saw 100ft of river wall demolished down to the foreshore. The temporary repairs here required 2,400 sandbags laid in a line running between whatever surviving walls could be made use of. This took some 300 man hours, and was built between 19 and 29 September 1940. Permanent repairs had to wait until the end of May 1941 and took rather longer, at just over seven months. This site is now part of the southern abutment of the Thames Barrier, built to protect London from flooding: it is thus possible that one of the Thames-Flood team's major incidents lay under what was once the Thames Barrier Education Centre.

### TF20 Royal Arsenal Co-operative Society

A bomb destroyed 50ft of the river wall and parapet on 18 October 1940. Some 800 sandbags were stacked around the breach and through the building on the landward side between 21 and 25 October. This task took 170 man hours. The owners later built a line of sheet piles across the crater to form a new temporary flood defence, to which walls of sandbags were added at either end, returning to the riverfront. This structure was retained for some time, although the sandbags were renewed between April and May 1945; the original 'temporary' sandbag wall thus seems to have served for more than four years.

### TF36 Badock's Wharf

On 27 December 1940 a bomb exploded on the foreshore, destroying much of Badock's Wharf and the concrete flood defence wall. The public footpath

T-F incident no. 36, Badock's Wharf: repair work under way in 1941, three months after a bomb strike on the flood defences in Greenwich. (© *LMA: TDP, P. Kennedy*)

in this area lay on the landward side of the wharf and was undamaged. The photo shows the scene in March 1941, just after the permanent repair programme implemented by the owners had begun. The site has been fenced off, and some of the timberwork for the new wharf has been stacked on the waterfront. However, rubble from the demolished buildings is still piled up on the foreshore, from where it was presumably removed by barge. The reinstatement was completed by 14 June 1941, three months later.

### TF64 Deptford Wharf

The photo shows the destruction of a 40ft length of river wall in May 1940 at the Southern Railway's Deptford Wharf. The temporary repairs here take the form of timber walling rather than sandbags, as can be seen behind the bomb damage. The timber parapet forming the heightened defences along the rest of the wharf can also be seen. Steel sheet piling was then used to retain the unstable ground around the crater, after which the river wall was rebuilt by 3 March 1942.

### TF97 Talbot's Wharf

On 17 October 1940, the building forming the flood defence was destroyed by HE to well below the standard level for a length of more than 30ft. Temporary repairs began in November, and were undertaken in March and June 1941. By December scouring was proving a problem, requiring work that was not completed until March 1942, with the permanent repair commencing a year later in February 1943.

T-F incident no. 64, Deptford Wharf. Bomb damage to the river wall at Deptford: the unstable frontage required a major rebuild, which took ten months to complete. (© *LMA: TDP, P. Kennedy*)

T-F incident no. 97, Talbot's Wharf: Percy Talbot's barge repair yards in 1937.
(© *Museum of London: PLA Collection 322653*)

## TF100 Ship Hotel, Greenwich

The destruction of the Ship Hotel also saw considerable damage to the water-front parapet and railings adjacent to the river stairs. Initially sandbags were used to remedy the situation, but this temporary dam was 'interfered with' on a number of occasions, calling for more permanent measures.

## Trafalgar House

Study of the riverfront in the Greenwich area has identified sites which have all the attributes of 1940s' bomb-damage repair, but are not recorded as 'incidents' in the T-F log books. One such is adjacent to the Trafalgar House, known to have been struck by a V-1 rocket in 1944, the blast also damaging the neighbouring waterfront properties. The river wall here exhibits brick and

T-F incident no. 100, Ship Hotel, Greenwich. Built in 1858 to a design by Philip Hardwick, the hotel is shown in 1937 before it was bombed. It sat next to the Garden Stairs, where watermen's skiffs could be hired by river workers before the war. (© *Museum of London: PLA Collection 322655*)

Detail of waterfront repairs next to the *Trafalgar*. (*TDP*)

concrete patching not inconsistent with a relatively hurried repair programme. If this is a direct response to a rocket strike on the river wall, then
why was this incident not reported to the T-F unit, or not recorded by them
in the official log book?

The answer may lie in the fact that the local Tunnel Avenue depot had been
closed for nearly three years by this date. The correct procedure for reporting
damage to the river wall in Greenwich in 1944 was to inform the Southwark
Park T-F or Pyrimont Wharf depots. Perhaps, in the very considerable heat
of the moment, this particular part of the Emergency Measures package was
overlooked on this occasion; the owners of the properties, appreciating the
potential danger, relied on common sense and local resources. Whatever
the reasoning behind the omission of this river wall repair from LCC's log
books, it raises the question of how many more patches of shuttered concrete
might represent breaches that are not enumerated in the 'official' statistics.
Certainly the modern foreshore survey has identified 1940s'-style repairs on
several sites that are not listed in the recorded work of the T-F team. While
this might represent general maintenance on the river wall in the 1950s, it
could also suggest that the Thames defences were actually breached more
often than the 122 incidents formally reported. Perhaps London was saved
from flooding even more times than LCC reported.

*Chapter Eight*

# City Quays

The City itself, the so-called 'Square Mile' that sat at the heart of the banking and mercantile sectors, suffered very heavy raids; most infamously that of 29 December 1940, when a massive fire storm destroyed acres of offices, the Guildhall and six Wren churches. Tower Bridge, London Bridge, Southwark Bridge and Blackfriars Bridge were all closed off, and no bus services were running anywhere in the City as the roads were pot-holed and blocked by mountains of debris. Somehow, St Paul's survived, thanks to good fortune and to a dedicated army of fire-watchers and fire-fighters. Somehow the river-front wall also survived, more or less undamaged, throughout most of the first phase of the Blitz. Then, in May 1941, all that changed when the last large, concerted attacks on the City destroyed vast areas of warehousing and offices. Indeed the majority of the potential breaches of the river wall here share the same date, the night of 10/11 May.

The potential for widespread flooding, however, is much less on the north bank of the river, where the land rises steeply beyond Thames Street, than in low-lying Southwark. As a consequence, the Thames-Flood team had less urgent work to do here. Several of the incidents involved the burning of

Peace in our time? The City viewed from Bankside in 1930.
(© *Museum of London: George Reid, 139349*)

## Incidents Attended in the City

| | | |
|---|---|---|
| TF49 | Castle Yard, Upper Thames St | March 1941 |
| TF79 | Three Cranes Wharf, Upper Thames St | May 1941 |
| TF80 | Red Lion Wharf, Upper Thames Street | May 1941 |
| TF82 | City & Continental Wharf, Upper Thames St | May 1941 |
| TF85 | Old Swan Wharf, Upper Thames Street | May 1941 |
| TF86 | City Commerce Wharf, Upper Thames St | May 1941 |
| TF87 | Tennant's Wharf, Upper Thames St | May 1941 |
| TF95 | Dowgate Wharf, Upper Thames St | May 1941 |
| TF96 | Bell Wharf, Upper Thames St | 1941 |

Burned out: city waterfront after the raid on 10/11 May. (© *Mary Evans Picture Library, 10078350*)

High explosives. Waterfront warehouses at Victoria Wharf in Puddle Dock, 1940.
(© *LMA: Cross & Tibbs 35617*)

Fires were started: battling with incendiary bombs at Blackfriars, October 1940.
(*Mary Evans Picture Gallery:* © *London Fire Brigade 10731946*)

Bomb damage: waterfront warehouses at Castle Baynard Wharf, May 1941.
(© *LMA: Cross & Tibbs 35370*)

moveable timber dams (or tide boards), used to block passageways, doorways and windows in warehouses that lay at or just below the highest tidal levels. The timberwork could be replaced relatively easily, once the small matter of the raging inferno had been put out. Other incidents involved the demolition of seriously-damaged waterfront warehouses, where the front wall also served as the river wall. Sometimes, during over-enthusiastic site clearance, rather too many courses of brickwork were removed to below the standard level, but the Thames-Flood inspectors were quickly on hand to remedy the situation. For the most part, the Corporation of London undertook most of the work, with support from the T-F team from Southwark Park.

Just beyond Southwark Bridge are traces of the repair to a modest breach in the river wall at Bell Wharf (TF96), again dating to the attack on 10 May 1940. It is now filled with a patch of concrete some 6ft across, but the river wall here has been heightened significantly over the last seventy years, thus the repair is no longer at the top of the modern parapet.

Once the burned-out waterfront warehouses were demolished and the sites cleared, the first line of flood defence then became the parapet; often the lowest courses of the old warehouse patched up and thickened with concrete. The most obvious example still surviving today lies directly to the east of Trig Stairs (Millennium Bridge), the former site of Castle Yard (TF49). Here the 1940s' patched-up parapet can be seen immediately below the late-twentieth-century works.

Although the river wall itself seems to have survived relatively unscathed in the City, its waterfront warehousing, however, suffered rather more, as LCC's bomb-damage maps show. By the end of the war, most of the build-ings between what was then St Paul's Station (now Blackfriars) and St Benet's church were burned out or blown up, as was everything between Southwark Bridge and London Bridge (including the great roof over Cannon Street Station).

The bridges in the City reach were also hit: Blackfriars was closed for two days after two direct hits from HE bombs, while Southwark Bridge suffered six incidents; the worst, unsurprisingly, in May 1941 when its northern arches were damaged, forcing closure for eight weeks. At one stage there was also an extensive crater on its northern approach road as well as a large UXB (unexploded bomb) at its southern end. London Bridge (now replaced) suf-fered blast damage in 1940 and 1944 but not serious enough to close it for any length of time. As for Tower Bridge, there were nine incidents, of which two were particularly serious. The first, in 1940, was a direct hit on the high-level span, the second involved very serious blast damage following the explosion of a large parachute mine on the foreshore in April 1941. This damaged a bascule, the towers and the engine-room.

(*Above*) TF96 Bell Wharf, Vintry. Below the life-belt on the modern guard rail and modern heightenings of the parapet is a concrete repair patch to a river wall breach that extends below the high water mark of 1941. (*TDP*)

(*Opposite, above*) TF49 Castle Yard. To the east of Trig Stairs (Millennium Bridge), the shuttered concrete repair of demolished waterfront warehouse foundations formed the new riverfront parapet in 1941, seen here in 2018 in a wide-angle panoramic view below modern heightenings. (© *TDP, A. Broomfield*)

(*Opposite, below*) TF49 Castle Yard: view showing the eastern end of Castle Yard, with 1941 repairs clearly visible below the modern 1970s' parapet. (© *TDP*)

Tide mark. This 1949 view shows the standard level of river defences achieved by blocked windows, stair-heads and the footings of demolished warehouses all brought up to the appropriate height. Castle Yard is in the cleared area in the centre of the photo. (*Unknown photographer*)

Shrapnel scars, probably from a V-1 rocket that exploded on the foreshore on 13 June 1944, can still be seen on Tower Wharf itself, around the entrance to 'Traitors' Gate'. This may have been one of the very first such weapons to land on London. Edward Hunter, on Home Guard duty at the Custom House, saw what he thought was a low-flying aircraft on fire, which suddenly crashed and exploded. Had the powerful 1,870lb charge struck the medieval quay wall itself, then the Tower would have been flooded.

Just to the east was Tower Pier, newly built in 1929 as the busy terminus for the pleasure boat trade. Ten years later it became the riverside Headquarters of the Harbour Service, the body that coordinated much of the war effort on the Thames, including the complexities of the Dunkirk evacuation in 1940. Subsequently it provided assistance to more than 400 ships that were sinking, stranded, collided, on fire or had lost their anchors. They also endeavoured to mark all wrecks and other underwater obstructions to improve navigation on the crowded river; such was the intensity of destruction on the tideway that they temporarily ran out of the required green bunting used to mark the wreck locations. The River Emergency Service, with its fourteen ambulance vessels and associated tenders, was also operated by them.

Regrettably, Tower Pier was destroyed by a direct hit on that dreadful date, 10 May 1941, with many killed and injured. Its loss was keenly felt, but the

Tower Wharf. Near miss: shrapnel scars on the river wall at Traitor's Gate, the Tower of London. Had the blast from the exploding V-1 rocket breached the wall, the Tower would have been flooded. (© *TDP*)

Brewer's Quay: pre-war image showing the busy City wharf, with ships, barges and rowing boats on the river. (© *Museum of London: PLA Collection 374722*)

Battered and bruised: the city, badly scarred but tidied up in 1941 after the punishing Blitz. View from the burned-out All Hallows Church to the derelict Brewer's Quay on the Thames. (© *LMA: Cross & Tibbs 36692*)

Harbour Service moved their principal station to Westminster Pier to continue their important work.

Another jetty that seems to have suffered during the Blitz was that next to Custom House; the battered remains of the lower timberwork are now sealed beneath a modern jetty platform, but survey of the foreshore in the immediate vicinity has revealed a number of vessel hulks here, all of which seem to have been abandoned in or by the mid-twentieth century. It is not too fanciful to see these boats as further evidence of the Blitz on the river. In summary, although the City's waterfront wall was not significantly breached, the wider waterfront and riverscape with its warehouses, bridges, jetties and river craft were far less fortunate.

PART THREE

# CONTAINMENT AND CONTINGENCIES

# Chapter Nine

# Emergency Services

## Protecting London's River

When seen from a bomber attacking the city by night or day, the great river provides too obvious a target, with its shipping, its wharves, its warehouses and its power stations. Consequently the Thames and its riverside communities suffered disproportionally during London's Blitz. Its especial vulnerability was recognized, not just by the establishment of LCC's Thames-Flood unit, but by the expansion of the other river-based teams, all of whom must have worked alongside them at the incidents attended. The River Police patrols, for example, were frequently the first to spot a potential river wall breach, or were the authority most likely to pass on relevant information received from other sources, as the T-F log books show. Their headquarters in Wapping was but 50 yards from Eagle Wharf (TF94) where the riverfront warehouse was destroyed on 14 March 1941, for example.

The ARP teams would also have observed damage to the river wall: there were many observation posts along the Thames, and the TDP team recorded what may prove to be the last example of its type at Tripcock Ness, affording fine views of the river as it flowed between the prime targets of Woolwich Arsenal and Silvertown. It was thus the police and the ARP units who served as the eyes (and ears) of the T-F teams: it was their messages, by phone, bicycle or motorbike, that triggered the required response.

## Fireboat Stations on the River

As for the Auxiliary Fire Service (AFS), their teams must certainly have been in attendance at many of the sites where the T-F worked; indeed, unless the fires could be extinguished, breaches could not be blocked. Some of the fires in waterfront warehouses could be tackled from the landward side, but many would require an attack from the river. In central London, there were ten river stations in operation during the height of the Blitz. These were initially part of the Auxiliary Fire Service, but in 1941 became part of the National Fire Service's River Division, later known as the River Thames Formation (RTF). Each station would comprise offices and the fire-fighters' dormitory and canteen. This would either be in an accommodation barge moored on the river or usually in a requisitioned school or commercial building on dry land.

Tried and tested: the emergency services in London had seen action before the war at major incidents such as this one at Colonial Wharf in 1935.

(*Mary Evans Picture Gallery: © London Fire Brigade 10793615*)

*Modus operandi*: fighting fires from the river at Wapping in 1935.
(*Mary Evans Picture Gallery*: © *London Fire Brigade 10793616*)

Access to the fire-boats often required a short pier with a floating pontoon, sometimes with one or two small offices/store buildings on it.

The vessels moored here were all painted battleship grey and comprised a range of types. First there were the fire-floats with their powerful monitors to direct a concentrated jet of water at a riverside fire. Of these, the *Massey Shaw* is the last survivor of its class, but in the 1940s was supported by vessels such as *James Braidwood*, *Beta III* and later *Diamond*. Other fire-floats were converted from naval vessels, and were subsequently returned to the Admiralty

Tower Pier, a pleasure boat embarkation point in 1937, became a hub for the river emergency services during the war before it suffered a direct hit. (© *Museum of London: PLA Collection 320944*)

In the thick of it: the police played many vital roles during the London Blitz.
(*Mary Evans Picture Gallery:* © *London Fire Brigade 10193282*)

Eyes and ears: for the T-F teams, the first news of waterfront breaches often came from river police patrols operating from their headquarters at Wapping, seen here in 1937.
(© *Museum of London: PLA Collection 321967*)

Head Office: the London fire brigade's new Lambeth HQ in 1940. The River Formation operated from the floating pontoon on the Thames.
(*Mary Evans Picture Gallery:* © *London Fire Brigade 10534485*)

Fire-floats were based at several Thames-side pontoons, such as this one at Cherry Garden, Bermondsey. (© *Museum of London: PLA Collection 322754*)

when hostilities ceased. Then there were the water-relay barges: these carried a series of pumps designed to relay water from the river via long extension hoses or branches to fire crews tackling blazes on shore. Indeed, much of the River Division's work involved the supply of water from the Thames to the teams on land, where bombs had fractured the mains and hydrants. Other vessels were used to tow obstructions or the relay barges, to serve as control centres at major waterfront incidents, or as floating canteens to support the active teams during their long ordeals.

By 1942, the River Formation's remit ran from Staines to the Nore, a distance of almost a hundred miles, but also included the River Medway as far as Queenborough. At its height there were some 1,500 personnel manning twenty-two stations with a fleet that included forty fire-boats of three types (river, esturial or seagoing) and forty-two water-relay barges.

There were some ten river stations concentrated in central London. The crews from three of these river stations would have worked with the Thames-Flood depot in Battersea. These included the London Fire Brigade's proud new headquarters, which still survives on the Albert Embankment at Lambeth (R2Z), with its pontoon directly in front of it. There was a temporary station at Battersea Bridge, in a former fire brigade building recently refurbished (R2Y), but subsequently demolished by 1966. This was just a few hundred yards from the River Formation's main Training School at Cheyne House next to Cadogan pier, on the opposite bank. The third station was based in a surviving riverfront building requisitioned from the London Rowing Club at

Putney (R2X), with the crews also making use of an accommodation barge moored nearby.

The Southwark Park T-F team would have had dealings with as many as five fire stations. On the south bank there was a station based at 73 Cherry Gardens (R4Z); although that building has gone, the pontoon still survives and its earlier reincarnation can be seen in the 1937 riverscape. All the waterfront buildings to the east of the pontoon were damaged during the Blitz.

An accommodation barge may have been utilized for Hay's Wharf station off Tooley Street (R3X); again the waterfront buildings here all suffered major damage, while just to the east, Mark Brown's Wharf site (TF78) was one of the larger T-F challenges that would have required collaboration between the two teams. Again, a similar story can be told at the South Wharf fire station (R4Y), initially housed in the former Fever Hospital buildings. This location was itself badly bombed (and the neighbouring river wall seriously breached; see TF21 and TF22), forcing crews to seek new accommodation at the nearby Pageant Wharf fire station. Indeed, even their jetty was hit by two V-1s.

On the north bank, there were two more stations to protect the City itself. Both were based in elegant late-Victorian offices that somehow survived the Blitz. One had its offices at 2A Eastcheap, near Billingsgate (R3Y). The building still survives at the head of Fish Street Hill, the lane that leads directly downhill to Billingsgate. The remains of the associated jetty that once accessed the pontoon may still be seen beneath the suspended Billingsgate Walkway, down on the foreshore. The buildings immediately to its west were blown up by a V-1 rocket, an act that may have damaged the pontoon itself.

The other City station was at 9 Carmelite Street (R3Z), with its associated jetty and pontoon off the Victoria Embankment just upstream of Blackfriars Bridge. An auxiliary pumping station stood next to it, the last survivor (until 2013) of the forty-four such facilities built in 1940 to pump water from the Thames at all states of the tide to hydrants that were more easily accessible to land-based fire crews. Many of these were erected over the river up against bridges, including Battersea, Lambeth, Westminster, Blackfriars, Southwark, Cannon Street and London Bridge itself. Gillian Crossan from the Thames Discovery Programme noted that there was also one attached to the railway bridge near Strand on the Green, while other members of the team have provisionally identified the neglected remains of two more auxiliary pumping stations. Both of these were set on major jetties built over the low tide line, one at Convoy's Wharf in Deptford and one at Charlton.

In Greenwich, the T-F Tunnel Avenue depot's nearest river fire station was based in requisitioned rooms in the Curlew Rowing Club (R4X); the jettied balcony on the river side of the current building has been replaced with concrete supports, although one solitary wooden post may represent the original

The City itself was served by two river-based fire stations; this one is at Blackfriars, with the *Massey Shaw* drawn alongside. (*Mary Evans Picture Gallery:* © *London Fire Brigade 10534545*)

1940s structure. An all-too-familiar litany records that a V-1 rocket badly damaged the neighbouring buildings as well as the waterfront wall itself, as is clearly shown in the repair work still visible in the river wall next to the Trafalgar Inn.

On the opposite bank of the Thames at North Woolwich, the R4W station worked closely with the Pyrimont Wharf T-F team. The fire crew once had offices in the Elizabeth Street School, a building just off Pier Road shown on the LCC Bomb Damage maps as 'Damaged Beyond Repair'. Given that the fire stations were manned twenty-four hours a day, there must have been casualties here. Indeed, as this chapter all too clearly shows, well over half of the river-based fire-fighting units were themselves bombed out. As for the Elizabeth Street station, there is no trace of it, although the pontoon used by the fire-boats survived until *c.*1986. Edwin Hunt recalls that, in happier times before the war, his family took him to that very same pier to board the paddle-steamer *Golden Eagle* for a week's holiday in Margate.

Just as the Thames-Flood teams were wound down as the threats posed by bomb and rocket attacks diminished, so too were the River Formation units. They gradually dwindled from twenty-two NFS stations to a peacetime three,

A long-disused auxiliary pumping station on the quay at Charlton. Note the pipework at the low-tide mark. (*TDP, N. Cohen*)

An auxiliary pumping station on the railway bridge near Strand-on-the-Green in *c*.1950; note pipework to draw water to hydrants on the bridge itself. (*TDP, G. Crossan*)

with the formation of the London Fire Brigade in 1948. Although this was the same number that served the City in 1939, only one of those original stations (Lambeth) was still operative, with South Wharf and Woolwich taking over from Blackfriars and Bermondsey.

## Fire-boat Stations on the Thames
### (Based on W. Hickin, *Fire Force*, 2013)

**Pre-war River-based Fire Stations**
Lambeth: Albert Embankment, SE1
Blackfriars: 9 Carmelite Street, EC4
Bermondsey: 73 Cherry Garden Street, SE16

**NFS River Division 1941–1942** (incorporating AFS stations)
R1Z   Richmond: Landsdowne House, 77–9 Petersham Road
R1Y   Barnes: 31 The Terrace, SW13
R1X   Teddington: Public Draw Dock, Ferry Road
R1W   East Molesey: Landing Stage, Hampton Court Bridge (south)
R1V   Sunbury: TV Skiff Club, Clarkes Wharf, Thames Street
R2Z   Lambeth: Albert Embankment, SE1
R2Y   Battersea: Battersea Bridge, SW11
R2X   Putney: London Rowing Club, SW15
R3Z   Blackfriars: 9 Carmelite Street, EC4
R3Y   Billingsgate: 2a East Cheap, EC3
R3X   Hay's Wharf: Tooley Street, SE1
R4Z   Bermondsey: 73 Cherry Garden Street, SE16

Fire service river tender R4Z no. 3. (*Mary Evans Picture Gallery:* © *London Fire Brigade 10534938*)

Fire-boat R4Z no. 19. (*Mary Evans Picture Gallery: © London Fire Brigade 10534939*)

R4Y   Rotherhithe: South Wharf, Rotherhithe Street, SE16
R4X   Greenwich: Curlew Rowing Club, SE10
R4W   North Woolwich, Elizabeth Street School, E16
R4V   Erith, British Plaster Board Works
R5Z   Grays, TS 'Exmouth', Essex

**River Thames Formation: March 1943–November 1944**
(A = Up-River Division; B = Down-River Division)

| | | | |
|---|---|---|---|
| A1Z | Richmond | A1Y | Barnes |
| A1X | Teddington | A1W | Molesey |
| A1V | Sunbury | A1U | Walton |
| A2Z | Lambeth | A2Y | Battersea |
| A2X | Putney | A3Z | Blackfriars |
| A3Y | Billingsgate | A3X | Hay's Wharf |

B1Z   Cherry Garden          B1Y   South Wharf
B1X   Greenwich              B1W  N. Woolwich
B1V   Erith
B2Z   Tilbury (annexes at Purfleet & Thameshaven)
B2Y   Greenhithe             B2X Southend
B2W  Queenborough (initially Port Victoria, then Sheerness)
B2V   Holehaven (annexe at Shellhaven)

*Beta III* moored close to fire station RZ4 at Cherry Garden Pier.
*(Mary Evans Picture Gallery: © London Fire Brigade 10534940)*

## Probable NFS River Thames Formation: November 1944
(A = Up-River Division; B = Down-River Division)

| | | | |
|---|---|---|---|
| A1Z | Richmond | A1W | Molesey |
| A1U | Walton | A2Z | Lambeth |
| A2Y | Battersea | A2X | Putney |
| A3Z | Blackfriars | A3Y | Billingsgate |
| A3X | Hay's Wharf | | |

| | | | |
|---|---|---|---|
| B1Y | South Wharf | B1X | Greenwich |
| B1W | N. Woolwich | B1V | Erith |
| B2Z | Tilbury (annexe at Purfleet) | B2Y | Greenhithe |
| B2X | Southend | | |
| B2W | Queenborough (initially Port Victoria, then Sheerness) | | |
| B2V | Holehaven (annexe at Shellhaven) | | |

## Probable NFS River Thames Formation: May 1945

| | | | |
|---|---|---|---|
| A3 | Lambeth | A5 | Putney/Hammersmith |
| A1 | Blackfriars | B9 | South Wharf |
| B7 | N. Woolwich | B1 | Tilbury |
| B3 | Southend | B2 | Queenborough |
| B4 | Holehaven | | |

## Overseas Contingent: 1944–45
Nos 1 and 2 Flotillas: Parent Ship, 5 × Fire-boats: 55 all ranks

## August 1945 NFS, River Thames Formation
Six fireboats plus control boat at Lambeth:

| | | | |
|---|---|---|---|
| RTF1 | Hammersmith | RTF2 | Lambeth |
| RTF3 | Blackfriars | RTF4 | South Wharf |

RTF5  North Woolwich          RTF6  Tilbury
RTF7  Holehaven

## 1947 NFS, River Thames Formation

| 1A | Lambeth | 1 | Blackfriars |
| 2 | South Wharf | 3 | Woolwich (from N. Woolwich) |
| 4 | Tilbury | | |

## 1948 London Fire Brigade: River Service

Lambeth, South Wharf, and Woolwich

*Chapter Ten*

# Bridges in the Blitz

## Keep London Moving

In 1938, Sir Harold Scott (Chief Administrative Officer for London Region) drew up plans for the city's response to the impending war. Regional chiefs were appointed to coordinate the fire and ambulance services and, from the staff of LCC, Major Bax (chief surveyor) became Regional Head of Rescue Services. Peirson Frank (LCC's Chief Engineer) now took over responsibility not just for the Thames-Flood team, but also for its buildings (not least County Hall itself, which suffered severe bomb damage), its utilities and also its roads and bridges. Unless emergency services, food supplies and public transport could move (more or less) freely, London would quite literally be bombed to a standstill. Each borough therefore appointed full-time road-repair teams; indeed, it was from these units that the T-F labour force was temporarily recruited, as and when required. Their main work was therefore to clear debris and make good the many craters that threatened to paralyse the city streets after each and every raid. After the Great Fire Storm of 29 December 1940, for example, City streets were 4ft thick with rubble, all of which had to be cleared at speed. When the Blitz was at its height, unexploded bombs, craters in the roads and damage to electricity substations severely restricted the operations of London's tram and trolleybus services. For a while, a passenger river-boat service was set up between Woolwich and Westminster. The journey time proved too long, however, not helped by delays caused by mines in the river, and the service was withdrawn six weeks later as the roads were repaired.

With regard to keeping the traffic flowing, Peirson Frank is perhaps best remembered for his handling of the 150ft crater at Mansion House. On 11 January 1941, a high-explosive bomb ripped Bank Underground Station apart. This was right in the middle of the City's busiest road junction, where seven major roads converge. First, two temporary bridges were laid across the site, one 100ft long, the other 50ft long; this work allowed the Lord Mayor to re-open the junction to traffic on 3 February, just three weeks later. Meanwhile, work continued around the clock to reinstate the site and the temporary bridges were removed on 29 March, only eleven weeks after the bomb strike. Such a schedule at such a time (there was little let-up in the Luftwaffe's

Temporary repairs to the Deptford Creek Bridge (badly damaged in 1940) were not replaced until the 1950s. (© *LMA 234561*)

operations) is nothing short of miraculous when set alongside the endless road-repair schedules that today's Londoners seem to endure.

## Tunnels under the Thames

The steady movement of London's traffic in wartime was thus one of many key concerns of LCC. Considerable planning was required, and thought was given to the crucial Thames crossing-points, the tunnels and bridges that provide the vital links for the twin-bank settlement. New floodgates were installed in the Rotherhithe and Blackwall tunnels, for example. The Blitz on Rotherhithe Tunnel began on 7 September 1940, when an incendiary bomb dropped down Shaft 2; barges moored close to it were also blown up, showering debris down the shaft. HEs exploded near the southern entrance on 29 December 1940, and the spiral stairs in Shaft 3 were damaged on 10 May 1941. The Blackwall Tunnel suffered bomb damage at both its northern and southern approaches, destroying the parapet walls, but was otherwise unscathed. Both tunnels therefore continued in operation with minimal disruption for the duration.

The complex work on the London Underground network has already been discussed, where twenty-five massive floodgates were installed in the tunnels below the river by the London Passenger Transport Board. The gates were closed during heavy raids (there is anecdotal evidence that occasionally trains were trapped in them) to seal off the vulnerable sections. That £1m investment paid off on the night of 9 September 1940 when the Strand-Charing Cross Loop tunnel took a direct hit, but the flood waters were contained. This proved to be the only London Underground tunnel that was so breached; by good fortune, this section of the network had been decommissioned just four years previously and thus its loss was not keenly felt.

## Bridges over Troubled Water

As for those vital transport arteries, the Thames bridges, it was noted in 1940 that the unstable Chelsea Bridge had been replaced with a rather stronger version, opened in 1937, while Wandsworth Bridge had also been rebuilt and widened so that it could now accommodate buses. Its opening was delayed by steel shortages until 20 September 1940, and since the war had already begun with a vengeance by that date, it was painted in camouflage blue-grey. The old Waterloo Bridge had just been demolished, and a temporary bridge installed while the ultra-modern replacement was being built. The subsequent fate of Central London's bridges during the Blitz is summarized below, but first a study of London's forgotten Emergency Bridges will be presented.

Working with records from the LCC Chief Engineer's office (in the London Metropolitan Archives), study of old aerial photography, Pathé News footage and reports in *The Times* newspaper, another neglected story from the Blitz was discovered by the FROG team some ten years ago. It concerns LCC's plan to the build three new 'emergency' bridges across the Thames, as a precaution in case the main bridges should suffer serious damage. These were built simultaneously by Holloway Brothers, starting in 1940 to the same basic design incorporating timber piling supporting steel girders for the decking, and thus similar to the temporary bridge erected alongside Lambeth Bridge during its reconstruction (1928–32) and that erected alongside Waterloo Bridge during its rebuilding (1936–42).

In the event, in spite of many direct hits and near misses, none of the 'old' bridges was destroyed, and the three Emergency Bridges were duly dismantled in or by 1948. This is not to say that the precautionary plan itself was necessarily wrong: nobody could predict with any accuracy how sustained or how damaging the Luftwaffe could be. With hindsight we now know that the very worst of the raiding was over by May 1941, but the spans of Emergency Bridges were not completed until the end of 1942, and new crossings not fully operative until the following year. That these particular precautionary measures were never put to the test does not make them white elephants. Instead the plan itself is seen as another example of the depth of detailed

Emergency Bridges: in addition to completing Waterloo Bridge, LCC engineers repaired bomb damage to all London's bridges and even built three new Emergency Bridges. This example, photographed in 1942, ran from their HQ at County Hall to Whitehall.
(© *LMA: LCC Photo Library 236871*)

pro-active planning undertaken by LCC in this period. That the Emergency Bridges were never put to full use – since no other bridges were ever out of action for a prolonged period – is best seen as a vindication of the efforts of London's anti-aircraft batteries and the RAF.

The Emergency Bridges served London until 1948, after which they were dismantled and, remarkably, sent off to the colonies to span rivers in Africa. One of the many memorable slogans that circulated during the war were the phrases 'make-do-and-mend' and 'waste not, want not', heartfelt pleas in a time of great scarcity. That the great steel structures from the Thames should have been put to such good use in far corners of the Empire surely represents an exemplary instance of recycling in an 'Age of Austerity'.

These major engineering exercises have left surprisingly little trace for latter-day archaeologists to record, in spite of the close attention of the TDP team. The spans were carried over the parapet level of the Embankment wall (rather than cutting down through it); arguably such a raised design renders the bridge more operable in the event of flooding caused by a river wall

Emergency Bridges, construction. Timber piles formed the piers (*above*) and laying the deck beams (*below*) for Emergency Bridge no. 3 (Battersea) in 1940. (© *LMA, 236830 & 236828*)

breach. However, it also means that there is next to no indication of the locations surviving as building scars on the present-day waterfront. With one possible exception, even the pile groups driven into the foreshore and riverbed seem to have been removed with remarkable thoroughness, leaving little to remind us of the tale of London's 'lost bridges', another largely unknown story of the Blitz.

**Emergency Bridge no. 1** ran from County Hall to the Victoria Embankment, thus linking LCC with Downing Street and the Ministry of Defence. The abutments would have been on the site of the present-day Millennium Wheel on one side and Whitehall Stairs/Horseferry Avenue on the other; as such it could have served as a potential replacement for Westminster Bridge, should that be destroyed. (More detailed information and relevant images are available online at: http://alondoninheritance.com/the-thames/ a-wartime-temporary-bridge-and-county-hall) There were three incidents concerning this bridge in the Blitz, all during its construction: an HE damaged the roadway decking and handrails; the bolt store and contractors' huts were destroyed by a parachute mine, showering the bridge with debris, while an

Emergency Bridges, construction. Preparing decking for Emergency Bridge no. 1 (County Hall) in 1942. (© *LMA, 236857*)

incendiary burned a large stack of timber being stored nearby for the bridge-works on 10 May 1941. County Hall itself suffered rather more damage, but this was later repaired. The Emergency Bridge was closed on 19 June 1947 and dismantled. It then took on a colonial role in the last decades of the British Empire, for it was shipped out to Northern Rhodesia to replace a pontoon over the Kafue River on the Great North Road. According to *The Times*, the bridge was officially declared opened on 2 April 1949 by Lady Beit and Sir Alfred Beit in the presence of the governor, Sir Gilbert Rennie, and Mr Creech-Jones, the Secretary of State for the Colonies. The 420ft span was erected on two piers (offering minimum obstruction to river traffic) and at a height of 9ft above the highest recorded flood levels.

**Emergency Bridge no. 2** was constructed in case either Vauxhall or Lambeth bridges were damaged. It ran from the Albert Embankment near Tinworth Street straight to the Tate Gallery (now Tate Britain) on Millbank. There was bomb damage to the capping of the river wall on the Albert Embankment side while the bridge was under construction; the blast also destroyed hand rails, four of the main piles, and sank the contractor's rowing boat. Another strike destroyed the contractor's accommodation and LCC's clerk of works' office. There is a Pathé News feature on the deconstruction of this bridge, a remarkable historical document, and also informative for those with a professional interest in Health and Safety at Work (Online at: https://thameshighway.wordpress.com/2015/01/18/londons-wartime-bridges). Taking advantage of one of the two highest Thames tides of the year on 28 March 1948, *The Times* reported that the 90-ton central span of the Mill-bank Bridge was floated out of position and laid up on floating pontoons next to the approach piers, where it was then dismantled. The bridge was bought by the Rhodesian government to span a tributary of the Zambezi River.

**Emergency Bridge no. 3** joined Battersea to Chelsea Embankment, and could have provided the Thames-Flood unit in Battersea Park with additional means of crossing the river should either Albert or Chelsea bridges be un-usable. The bridge ran from just outside the Stoneyard depot in the park across the river to the Embankment close to the junction with Royal Hospital Road. Unlike the other two 'temporaries', construction here was only but briefly interrupted, in this case by a UXB on the Battersea Park side. On 19 April 1948, *The Times* reported that the main span of the bridge was removed in an engineering operation which lasted less than four hours. This section, some 140ft long and weighing 92 tons, was lifted from its bearings by steel trestles in coupled barges, working with the rising tide. Two tugs then towed the barges to the Battersea shore, where the span was deposited on a temporary structure to await dismantling. The bridge components had been

Dismantling Emergency Bridges. Emergency Bridge no. 3, Millbank, in 1948. As the tide turns and starts to rise, two coupled barges with supporting steel trestles are towed under the central spans. Rising tide brings barge-mounted steel trestles in contact with the central span. (© LMA, 236877 & 236880)

Dismantling Emergency Bridges. Emergency Bridge no. 1 (County Hall) in 1948. At high tide, the power of the tidal river lifts the span free of piled piers, allowing a complete section to be towed clear ready for export to the colonies. All timber piles for the piers were withdrawn by crane, ensuring that no navigational hazards were left in the river. (© *LMA, 236184 & 236901*)

bought by the Crown Agents for the Colonies and were subsequently shipped to Uganda, where a new bridge was constructed to improve transport links in connection with the infamous groundnut scheme (1947–51) in neighbouring Tanganyika. (Online at https://alondoninheritance.com/the-thames/a-temporary-wartime-chelsea-bridge).

## The Main Thames Bridges
### (see also S. Croad, *London's Bridges*, 1983)

### Wandsworth Bridge

The old bridge (1873) was replaced by Peirson Frank's continuous lattice-girder design. Work commenced in 1935 to widen it to accommodate buses, but its opening was delayed by steel shortages until 20 September 1940. This was just a fortnight after the London Blitz had begun with a vengeance; consequently, it was painted in camouflage blue-grey. Arguably, this seems to have been a successful ploy since the bridge was not damaged.

### Battersea Bridge

The old eighteenth-century wooden Battersea Bridge was replaced in 1890 by the current bridge, to a design by Joseph Bazalgette, built by John Mowlem. Ironwork and masonry on the southern end of the bridge were damaged by two HEs on the night of 29 November 1940. Two pumping stations for the AFS were built alongside the bridge, one on the upstream side and one down-stream.

Battersea Bridge, showing wartime auxiliary pumping stations erected next to the second and fourth piers. These could draw water from the Thames at all states of the tide, pumped up the pipework to hydrants on the bridge itself. The fire station (with tower) can be seen on the Battersea bank. (© *LMA, 234489*)

## Albert Bridge

Opened in 1873, this most graceful but fragile of bridges famously asks troops crossing it to break step; clearly it would not have been robust enough to withstand close attention from the Luftwaffe. Since it and its sister bridge Chelsea (see below) were the prime routes for the Thames-Flood team based in Battersea Park to access the Chelsea/Westminster waterfront, Peirson Frank had Emergency Bridge no. 3 built alongside it. After the war, Albert Bridge enjoyed several repair campaigns, most notably in 1973 when two extra piers were added to support the weakened central span.

## Chelsea Bridge

Demolition of the original Chelsea Bridge (opened in 1858) began in 1935, and it was replaced by a new one in 1936–37, designed by Peirson Frank and built by Rendel, Palmer and Tritton. It was thus less than five years old when the Blitz began. There is still bomb scarring on the downstream face of the pier at the Battersea end, presumably associated with the strike that damaged that abutment. That apart, the bridge seems to have survived without any other major structural damage.

Chelsea Bridge: repairs to bomb-damaged abutment near North Carriage Drive, 1948. (© *LMA*)

Tell-tale signs: shrapnel scars on Chelsea Bridge pier, Battersea Park side. (*TDP*)

Detail of shrapnel scars on Chelsea Bridge pier, Battersea Park side. (*TDP*)

## Vauxhall Bridge

The current bridge was built in 1906 to a design by Maurice Fitzmaurice, W. Riley and Richard Norman Shaw. It replaced the first iron bridge to span the Thames, built 110 years earlier.

The bomb scarring on the Pimlico end on the bridge piers may represent blast damage from the major raid on 16/17 April 1941. This was witnessed by a local schoolboy called Eric Walker, presumably on fire-watching duty that night. He was particularly interested in the thirty figureheads that adorned

Vauxhall Bridge, 1941: (*Above*) Setting up an auxiliary pumping station on a pier. (*Below*) Work continues on the bridge as the *Massey Shaw* stands by.
(*Mary Evans Picture Gallery:* © *London Fire Brigade 10534719 & 10534721*)

Near miss: shrapnel scars on Vauxhall Bridge pier, Pimlico. (*TDP*)

Castle's Shipyard, located at Baltic Wharf next to the bridge. A single HE bomb damaged the offices at 11.00pm, and the rest of the wharf, buildings and figureheads were totally destroyed by three more bombs at 4.00am. If that wasn't enough, a V-1 exploded in the river at the north end of the bridge on 21 July 1944.

## Lambeth Bridge

The original Lambeth Bridge replaced the ancient horse ferry in 1862, but was soon in need of major repairs. This provided only temporary relief, and the decision to rebuild it was made in 1892. However, it still remained in use until further damaged by the 1928 flood disaster. Work on the new replacement began in 1929, after a temporary piled footbridge had been erected (one of the models on which the Emergency Bridges of 1940 were based). The main bridge was finally declared open in 1932, by which time Peirson Frank had taken over the LCC Chief Engineer's role from Sir Reginald Bloomfield. Two small auxiliary pumping stations were erected next to the piers on the upstream side.

Even more than the others, this bridge led a charmed life. On 15 November 1940, two HEs exploded either side of the abutment; although the Embankment parapet, lamps, paving and waterfront steps were damaged, the bridge itself escaped unscathed. A fortnight later, there was a direct hit in the centre of the Lambeth shore span, but luckily the bomb did not fully explode.

Lambeth Bridge bomb disposal in the 1940s: an unexploded bomb is removed. (*Mary Evans Picture Gallery: © Robert Hunt Library 10290571*)

## Westminster Bridge

The present bridge was opened in 1862, replacing Labelye's famous predecessor built in 1739–50. Its eastern abutment sat up against County Hall, where the LCC's Chief Engineer had his office. The western end passed the Houses of Parliament, a prime target hit fourteen times by the Luftwaffe, with the bombs on 10/11 May 1941 being particularly destructive. Another bomb, no doubt intended for the Palace of Westminster, breached the river wall in Victoria Tower Gardens (TF60). As for the bridge itself, it seems to have survived largely unscathed, although an unexploded bomb was dredged from the Thames close to it on 17 January 2017.

## Hungerford Footbridge

This bridge and its immediate neighbour **Charing Cross Railway Bridge** were both severely damaged by a V-1 doodlebug in 1944 that hit the fourth span; a similar weapon also damaged the nearby river wall next to Cleopatra's Needle (TF112). According to *The Times* of 7 April 1947, permanent repairs to the footbridge were not scheduled to be completed until 9 June 1947, and pedestrians were therefore advised to continue to use the Emergency Bridge near County Hall in the interim.

Charing Cross Bridge: removing a huge unexploded land mine from the railway tracks. Had the device exploded, the destruction would have been considerable.
(*Mary Evans Picture Gallery: © London Fire Brigade 10534657*)

Charing Cross Bridge: the land mine is lifted from the tracks onto a trolley and is rolled into the station. (*Mary Evans Picture Gallery:* © *London Fire Brigade 10534658 & 10794023*)

## Waterloo Bridge

This structure deserves a chapter of its own as its construction, which continued throughout the Blitz, was considered a national priority; Hitler's bombs weren't going to stop work on this elegant structure, although they came very close, very often. There were, in fact, two Waterloo Bridges, as a temporary iron bridge supported on timber piles had been erected to accommodate the traffic while the 'new' bridge was under construction. Taken together, they suffered more hits than any other bridge on the Thames.

An oil incendiary exploded on the decking of the 'new' bridge in September 1940, and a month later an HE hit the bridge but did not explode fully. The same raid saw damage to the stores of building materials and to the main crane on Canterbury Wharf. Two HEs in November hit both the north and south end of the bridge, injuring the night watchman and damaging the iron girders. The autumn of 1940 also saw several strikes on the adjacent temporary bridge, with damage to the footbridge as well as to the southern approach road, where an HE burst through into the vaults below. These premises were leased to a theatrical outfitter, and the damaged costumes had to be removed before repair work could begin.

Waterloo Bridge: dismantling the old Waterloo Bridge in 1934, with LCC's temporary bridge maintaining access alongside. (© *LMA, 236089*)

New Waterloo Bridge completed. Note the cleared bomb site on the South Bank (TF13) next to the Shot Tower, undeveloped in 1948 but earmarked for the Festival of Britain. (© *LMA, 236028*)

A serious strike in April 1941 damaged a pier, both arches and the timber footway, with a second strike two days later hitting the main girder on the east side. The bridge was re-opened for single-file traffic nine days later, the same day that the north end of the 'new' bridge took a direct hit when a bomb crashed straight through the decking on span 3. By some miracle, it didn't explode until it had fallen into the river below. The hole had been repaired by September of that year.

Somehow, Waterloo Bridge survived its personal, very intensive Blitz. It was opened initially to single-line traffic in 1942, a testament to the single-minded work force that famously included many women (hence its nickname 'the Ladies Bridge') since many of the original gang of able-bodied men had long since been conscripted.

As for Waterloo's temporary bridge, once dismantled, it enjoyed an active retirement. *The Times* of 24 November 1945 reports that it had been shipped out to Arnhem to span the Rhine, replacing the bridge destroyed in October 1944 during the bloody fighting between the advancing Allies and the stubborn German resistance. Dr J.A. Ringers, Minister of Public Works and Reconstruction at The Hague, declared that the bridge that had served Londoners during the Blitz would stand as a lasting symbol of the friendship between the two countries.

### Blackfriars Bridge

Joseph Cubitt's bridge was opened in 1869, replacing the first Blackfriars Bridge exactly 100 years after it had been built. Two auxiliary pumping stations were established in the river on the downstream side (i.e. between the

Blackfriars: the only wartime auxiliary pumping station in the City to survive into the twenty-first century (but now demolished). Just upstream of Blackfriars Bridge, it was next to the fire brigade's River Formation pontoon. Note the solid pipework at low tide level to draw the water up to street level. (*TDP*)

road and rail bridges) in addition to the one built alongside the fire brigade's pontoon alongside the Embankment. As with all the City bridges, those at Blackfriars must have presented tempting targets. The road bridge was damaged by two direct hits from HE bombs, but the damage cannot have been too severe since it was only closed for two days.

## Southwark Bridge
The First World War delayed the opening of the current Southwark Bridge, upon which work started in 1913 but was not completed until 1921. It was designed by Sir Ernest George and built by Mott, Hay and Anderson. The Second World War also impacted upon Southwark Bridge, which suffered six incidents, the worst being in May 1941. The northern arches were damaged, forcing closure for eight weeks.

Southwark Bridge: northern abutment, hit by an HE bomb in May 1941; view looking towards the City from the bridge. Note the total destruction of waterfront warehouses.
(© *LMA, Cross & Tibbs 35591*)

Dangerous driving: a bomb crater on the abutment of Southwark Bridge was larger than a fire brigade towing unit and trailer pump (the fire-fighters, driving at night, escaped with minor injuries). (*Mary Evans Picture Gallery:* © *London Fire Brigade 10534696*)

There was also an extensive crater on its northern approach road as well as a large UXB at its southern end, interfering with traffic flow. Two auxiliary pumping stations were constructed alongside the bridge, one next to the northern pier, one next to the southern, both on the upstream face.

## London Bridge

John and John Rennie (father and son) designed and then built the bridge that replaced the battered medieval structure in 1832. Two auxiliary pumping stations were erected in the river, both on the upstream side, one at the northern and one at the southern end. Although the bridge subsequently suffered blast damage in 1940 and 1944, it was not serious enough to close it for any length of time. It was the demands of post-war traffic that proved too much for it, and it was itself replaced between 1967 and 1973.

London Bridge: this century-old bridge, in the heart of the Pool of London in 1930, survived the war, but not the demands of modern traffic. (© *Museum of London: George Reid 001359*)

## Tower Bridge

Tower Bridge was built to the design of the City's architect Horace Jones by the engineer Sir John Wolfe-Barry between 1886 and 1894. Its world-famous profile must have made it one of the key landmarks that the Luftwaffe had in their sights. The double-leaf bascules had to be raised to allow shipping to access the Upper Pool and its dense concentration of wharves and warehouses

Tower Bridge standing sentinel over the City's working port in 1930, but a tempting target for enemy bombers. (© *Museum of London: George Reid 11928*)

Tower Bridge up top: close inspection by engineers of serious bomb damage to bascule lifting mechanisms on 8 October 1940. (© *LMA: Cross & Tibbs 36717*)

to the east of London Bridge. Consequently it was rather more than just an icon as it was a working part of the port. It suffered no less than nine incidents, two of which were particularly serious. The first, in 1940, was a direct hit on the high-level span: the hydraulic mains were severed, temporarily putting the bridge out of action. The second involved very serious blast damage following the explosion of a large parachute mine on the foreshore in April 1941. This damaged a bascule, the towers and engine-room. A third engine was installed in 1942 in case further attacks disabled the lifting mechanisms, but was removed in the 1970s when electricity replaced steam power.

## Abutment

London's bridges therefore survived the Blitz, by virtue of robust engineering, hard labour and good fortune. Given that the Thames was the principal feature that guided the Luftwaffe to their targets, it is perhaps surprising that they fared so well; clearly bomb-aiming was not a high-precision science in 1940. In addition to the bridges' near misses, the saga of London's unexploded bombs merits mention. Had everything that was dropped on the town exploded as per the instructions, perhaps things may have been a lot worse. The bridge chapter above notes at least five UXBs, a significant percentage of the total. It has been suggested that since many of the bombs were constructed by forced labour, the armament workers deliberately sabotaged a proportion of their output. If true, this brave act of defiance certainly saved some of London's bridges and much else besides.

To conclude, it is worth recording that the engineer with a major responsibility for the construction of the most bridges over the Thames is LCC's Peirson Frank: between 1930 and 1945, he oversaw the completion of no fewer than seven bridges (if our three emergency bridges are included); an average of one every two years. That would be quite an achievement if that was his sole occupation in peacetime, but that was not his sole occupation and this was not peacetime.

*Chapter Eleven*

# Secret Heroes

## The Saving of London

With masterful understatement, a summary report on the LCC's Chief Engineer's response to the Blitz states that 'all services for which the Department was responsible functioned, despite damage and dislocation due to enemy action.'

The bald statistics, stripped of the fire, choking smoke, shrapnel and human cost, record the number of 'incidents' to which his teams responded. These included the 122 breaches of the river wall, repairs to the Greenwich Foot Tunnel and 176 on bridges and other tunnels, as summarized in this book. However, their work also involved 1,383 incidents associated with public buildings and 530 rebuilding breakages to the main drainage and sewage systems. For the hard-pressed fire service, some forty temporary pumping stations were erected to relay water from the Thames at all states of the tide to hydrants on bridges and piers; 17 miles of 24in (60cm) steel pipework were laid under the streets, while static water tanks containing 14.5 million gallons of water were set up, as well as a further eighty reservoirs to supply another 250,000 gallons.

So how did London County Council's engineer perform all these feats of demolition, clearance, repair and reinstatement? To work on the utilities, he augmented his own 'civilian' staff by calling upon the newly-raised companies of Royal Engineers, some 4,000 men conscripted from Wimpey's, Costains, Constable & Hart, Nutall and Mowlem. For debris clearance, he brought in sixteen Pioneer companies, and raised the No. 2 Docks Group of the Royal Engineers, former dockers and stevedores. They were supported by motorized transport units, providing more than 200 lorries. During the period of the very worst of the bombing and its aftermath, from 1940 to 1941, he was thus able to call upon a 'Special Force' of some 13,000 men. The T-F team was thus one unit within a much larger para-military organization.

## Named Engineers

We know little about those who actually worked for the Thames-Flood-Prevention service, although a few names appear in the correspondence files, in the log books or in the incident reports. One of those whose name regularly

A civil engineer's war: one of LCC's T-F engineers (not in cloth cap) checks on a sandbag wall in 1940. (© *LMA: TDP, P. Kennedy*)

appears in the log books was clearly first on the scene of many incidents, and was listed as an 'Inspector Tatt'. Two of the key engineers who held permanent salaried positions with the T-F were T. Muir (£460 p.a.) and A.R. Vickers (£400 p.a.), while another group of seven engineers were paid weekly and therefore presumably formed part of a roster. They were R.S.B. Harvey (£8), N.F. Mackett (£7), C.J. Stanley Smith (£7.10s), G.M. Woodley (£6.15s), A.S. Henderson (£6), T.S.V. Rawlins (£6) and H.W. England (£5.15s). It is interesting to note that the wage differentials listed here show that a career structure was still evident in the civil engineer's office, in spite of the aerial mayhem dropping all around it.

## Unnamed Labourers

A record of pay scales for the working men suggests that the T-F labourers received £3.5s per week, rising to £3.15s per week for the foreman, still half the wage that an experienced professional engineer could anticipate. Some labourers were expected to work twenty-four hours on and then take twenty-four hours off, but were given an extra 1s per day meal allowance. We have, as yet, no recorded names for any of the labourers or lorry drivers who worked so hard on the waterfront sites to repair the breaches: the correspondence files regularly refer to them simply as 'Labour supplied by such-and-such a Borough'. However, Peter Kennedy uncovered a unique set of photographs in the London Metropolitan Archives: these were from the Glengall Wharf site and show one of the T-F teams in action on the Isle of Dogs. The men were almost certainly recruited locally, and most of them were probably too old for active service in the armed forces. On the home front, however, age, gender or non-combatant status counted for nothing.

## Knighthood

As for Thomas Peirson Frank himself, he was knighted in recognition of his wartime work as the 'Co-ordinating Officer for Road Repairs and Public Utility Services for the London area': the citation states that he 'personally directed the repair services that enabled London to carry on in spite of the severest air-raids'; the highly-complex organization he set up included the Thames-Flood Prevention Emergency Repairs service. He became president of the Institution of Civil Engineers (1945–46), but retired from LCC in July 1946. Not a man to seek a quiet retirement, he then became a consultant, working on sea defence works at Chesil Beach (Dorset) and on a flood prevention scheme in Salford (Lancashire). Broadening his horizons, he then put his considerable energies to work across the Commonwealth, with work on water storage for irrigation schemes in British Guiana, constructing four bridges in Nigeria, power stations in Malaya and Melbourne, not to mention a tunnel under the Thames at Long Ditton.

The survival of a set of papers relating to his wartime role as Chief Engineer for LCC suggests that he was considering writing up his memoirs, but unfortunately he died in November 1951 before a full account of his contribution to the war effort could be brought to publication. Although his Presidential Address to the Institution of Civil Engineers (ICE) does indeed make mention of the 'Thames-Flood' team, that aspect of his work is omitted in the official ICE obituary, published by them in January 1952. This book tries to make good that omission by showing the extent of the detailed planning and practical infrastructure that underpinned London's response to the Blitz. It was an integral part of a wider programme, without which the capital might not have survived the horror of a war waged against civilians.

## A Measure of Success

Thanks to the vision of people like Sir Peirson Frank, London had a plan to work with; thanks to its citizen army, London found the inner strength to implement it. Central London was flooded in 1928, there was serious flooding on the Thames to the west of the conurbation in 1947, and further devastating floods downriver in 1953. However, there were no major recorded inundations between 1940 and 1945, in spite of more than 100 bomb or rocket strikes on the river wall. That is surely testament enough to the vision, organization and proficiency of LCC's Thames-Flood team.

# PART FOUR

# NAUTICAL WARFARE

*Chapter Twelve*

# No Grave but the Sea

In the next chapters, the impact of the Second World War on the shipping that plied the Thames is discussed, taking an archaeological perspective where appropriate. The awful losses of ships and their 'civilian' crew during this period are graphically recorded in their evocative memorial on Tower Hill, London. It lists on panel after panel the names of all those merchant seaman and fishermen who have 'no grave but the sea'. It is worth recording that for assistance with mine-sweeping and patrol duties, the Royal Navy requisitioned some 1,700 small civilian vessels, many of them trawlers or other robust fishing boats, a service to the nation that saw 3,000 lives lost. As for the larger vessels, a regrettably high proportion of the merchant ships lost on the perilous Atlantic convoys were registered in London, a consequence of that port being the largest in the land, a point emphasized by the imposing scale of the adjacent building, once the prestigious HQ of the Port of London Authority itself. The impact of the war from fishing harbours to major port communities such as London and Liverpool was therefore profound and all-pervading.

Also it was not just in mid-Atlantic that the convoys suffered: many vessels were also wrecked in the Thames during the Blitz. A catalogue published by Richard and Bridget Larn (1996) provides the names of some 123 such casualties and an augmented version of this source is published here. A sample of those wrecks was recently rediscovered during the dredging of the Princes Channel in the outer estuary, investigated by divers from Wessex Archaeology working with the Port of London Authority, now published by Dr Anthony Firth and his team. Moving upstream to the River Medway, a major tributary of the Thames, a remarkable graveyard of abandoned naval and commercial craft including many barges and lighters was recorded in Whitewall Creek.

A third nautical assemblage – but this time comprising the remains of rather smaller vessels lost in the Blitz – was recorded by the Thames Discovery Programme on the foreshore in the heart of the City, as Eliott Wragg's contributions in 2017 to *The River's Tale* records. Taken together, these studies provide a reminder of the diverse vessels that worked the river and its wide estuary, serving the Port of London in its heyday. The range includes skiffs, trawlers, sailing barges, lighters, coastal steamers, colliers, tankers and ocean-going merchantmen, as well as the motor mine-sweepers and U-boat chasers that tried to protect them. That sample can be extended to include the remains of contemporary craft now abandoned in West London at Brentford and Isleworth, but also recorded by the Thames Discovery Programme.

## Perils of the Sea: Storms, Shoals, Mines, Bombs and U-boats

Coupled with infamous heavy weather in the North Sea, shipping on the east coast and Thames estuary also faced a ruthless onslaught from the Nazi war machine. By destroying vital supplies of imported food, fuel and military equipment, an island nation could be battered or starved into submission more easily than by invasion. Indeed, the level of UK losses in shipping, cargoes and crew in the first years of the conflict were frankly unsustainable. That was a war we were not winning. From 1939 to 1943, mines laid by U-boat or dropped by the Luftwaffe were the number one killer for Thames shipping. Extensive efforts were made to clear the approaches to the Port of London of these magnetic and acoustic mines, but this proved a dangerous task in itself, destroying nineteen naval mine-sweepers and many of their crew. Attacks by aircraft, such as the Stuka dive-bomber, also proved lethal on several occasions, but none were recorded after 1943. Arguably, the demands placed on the German war machine with the opening up of the Eastern Front in distant Russia did much to relieve the pressure on Britain and the shipping upon which the island economy depended. For all of 1944 and 1945, while the navy cleared or contained the mines and the RAF and AA batteries fought to maintain air superiority, there were but two losses caused by enemy action: the culprits were a V-1 rocket (a portent of a grim future), and a midget submarine.

## Losses in the Thames Estuary: September 1939 to May 1945

During the course of the war, some 2,000 convoys were brought down the east coast from as far north as the Firth of Forth to and from the Thames, or between London and ports to the south and west. However, in the first three months of the war, ships were being sunk in the Thames estuary at a rate of two or three every day, in spite of the normal mine-sweeping operations conducted by the Royal Navy, as the late Eric Rawlinson of the City Yeomanry recalled. Then, in November, a German flying boat was observed dropping items by parachute into the sea. One fell into shallow water and was recovered at low tide. It proved to be a new type of magnetic mine. These would lie on the seabed until activated by a ship passing overhead. These mines were not detected by the usual mine-sweeping methods then used by the navy. One of the countermeasures suggested was to shoot down or frighten off the enemy aircraft laying these magnetic mines. To facilitate this, six Bofors guns from the 32nd Battery of the City of London Yeomanry and a searchlight were mounted on requisitioned Thames paddle-steamers, three of which had already served as mine-sweepers during the Great War. They were the *Queen of Kent* (built 1916, 798 tons), the *Queen of Thanet* (built 1916, also 798 tons) and the *Thames Queen* (built 1898, 517 tons). They joined the 10th Mine-Sweeping Flotilla, and were tasked to patrol the estuary by day and anchor at night in the shipping lanes with the intention of shooting down German mine-laying aircraft. During the very cold weather, mines would float to the surface, obliging the crew to shoot and sink them, as shown in Eric Rawlinson's photograph. All three ships survived the war and returned to civilian life, but two had been scrapped by 1952; the fate of the *Thames Queen* is not recorded.

In spite of such valiant efforts by the mine-sweeping flotillas in the estuary, the magnetic and acoustic mines, U-boats and Luftwaffe bombers continued to take a heavy toll. In these listings (based on the 1996 catalogue published by Richard and Bridget Larn), the name of the vessel is followed (if known) by the date she was built, her gross tonnage (T), and her function or the cargo she

'Mine Kampf': 32 Battery City of London Yeomanry firing at floating mines in the Thames Estuary, December 1939. (© *Eric Rawlinson*)

carried. Where a vessel is shown with two different roles, it denotes one of the many civilian vessels requisitioned by the navy for e.g. mine-sweeping or coastal patrol duties. A similar system was in operation in the First World War; indeed, fifteen of the older vessels in our catalogue are recorded as having served in the previous conflict. The final columns note the number of crew members killed (ranging from 1 to 400+), followed by the cause and date of the wreck. It should be mentioned that navigation in the ever-changing tidal river was increasingly difficult in this period with fewer navigational aids and support; hence the significant number of wrecks foundering on semi-submerged mudflats, sandbanks and foreshores. The oldest vessel lost was HMS *Cornwall* (1815), some were launched in the late nineteenth century, but many were more recent having been built in the 1920s or 1930s, while two of the vessels were less than a year old.

## Losses in the Thames Estuary

### 1939

HMS *Blanche* (1930), Destroyer, T: 1,360, four lost, mine 13/11/1939.
SS *Ponzano*, T: 1,346, cargo: 1,180 tons from Valencia, mine 13/11/1939.
SS *Matra* (1926), T: 8,003, cargo: 5,750 tons from Baltimore, sixteen lost, mine 13/11/1939.
SS *Woodtown*, T: 794, cargo: 1,020 tons of granite from Newlyn, mine 15/11/1939.
*Mastiff* (1938), Trawler/Naval mine-sweeper, T: 520, mine 20/11/1939.
SS *Lowland* (1911), T: 974, cargo: coal from Blyth, nine lost, mine 22/11/1939.
SS *Hookwood* (1923), T: 1,537, cargo: coal from Blyth, two lost, mine 23/11/1939.
SS *Spaarnden* (1922), T: 8,857, cargo to Antwerp, mine 27/11/1939.
SS *Rubislaw*, T: 1,041, cargo: cement to Aberdeen, thirteen lost, foundered 28/11/1939.
SS *San Calisto* (1937), T: 8,010, Tanker en route to Hull, six lost, mine? 02/12/1939.
*Ray of Hope* (1925), Steam Drifter/Naval mine-sweeper, T: 98, mine 10/12/1939.

### 1940

*Eta*, Fishing vessel, T: 81, foundered 06/01/1940.
SS *Townley* (1923), T: 2,888, cargo: 4,300 tons of coal from Tyne, mine 07/01/1940.
*Truida*, T: 176, en route Holland to Rochester, foundered 09/01/1940.
SS *Josephine Charlotte*, T: 3,310, cargo: steel to Congo, four lost, mine 16/01/1940.
SS *Melrose*, T: 1,589, cargo: steel to Grangemouth, eighteen lost, foundered 15/03/1940.
*Maida* (1914), Trawler, T: 107, all crew lost, mine 16/03/1940.
SS *Capitaine Augustin* (1922), T: 3,137, en route from Rouen, two lost, mine 17/03/1940.
SS *Sint Annaland* (Netherlands), T: 2,248, foundered 17/03/1940.
SS *Tina Primo* (Italy), T: 4,853, en route to Genoa, one lost, foundered 18/03/1940.
SS *Okeania* (Greece), T: 4,843, en route to River Plate, one lost, foundered 08/04/1940.
SS *Hawnby* (1936), T: 5,404, cargo: coal to Gibraltar, mine 20/04/1940.
SS *Stokesley* (1922), T: 1,149, cargo: 1,600 tons, fifteen lost, mine 24/04/1940.
SS *Abukir* (1920), T: 675, cargo: troops etc. from Dunkirk, 400+ lost, torpedo 28/05/1940.
SS *Westella*, T: 413, en route from Dunkirk, U-boat torpedo 29/05/1940.
*Blackburn Rovers*, Trawler, T: 422, en route from Dunkirk, U-boat torpedo 31/05/1940.
SS *Hardingham* (1933), T: 5,415, cargo: 7,350 tons of coal, three lost, mine 08/06/1940.
*Myrtle* (1928), Trawler/Naval mine-sweeper, T: 550, mine 14/06/1940.

'Cold war': HMS *Queen of Kent* breaks the ice in the North Sea in January 1940 while on mine-sweeping duties. (© *Eric Rawlinson*)

MV *Sabier* (3,785 gross tonnage) was built in 1929 in Leningrad, USSR; seen here on one of her last visits to London in 1937 before she was sunk by the Luftwaffe.
(© *Museum of London: PLA Collection 322775*)

*Fleming* (1929), Trawler/Naval mine-sweeper, T: 358, bombed 24/07/1940.

*Staunton* (1908) (also requisitioned in Great War, 1914–20), Trawler/Naval anti-U-boat patrol, T: 358, thirteen lost, mine 28/07/1940.

SS *City of Brisbane* (1920), T: 8,006, cargo: 2,000 tons lead, eight lost, bombed 02/08/1940.

HMS *Tamarisk* (1925), T: 545, Naval mine-sweeper, bombed 12/08/1940.

*Pyrope* (1932), T: 295, Trawler/Naval mine-sweeper, bombed 12/08/1940.

MTB no. 15 (1939), T: 18, motor torpedo-boat, foundered 24/09/1940.

SS *Highwave*, T: 1,178, cargo: coal, foundered 30/09/1940.

*Scotch Thistle*, Drifter/Naval mine-sweeper, T: 84, foundered 07/10/1940.

*Aisha* (1934), Yacht/Harbour Defence Patrol, T: 117, mine 11/10/1940 (A. Firth et al, *London Gateway: Maritime Archaeology in the Thames Estuary*, p. 67, 2012).

*Resolvo* (1913) (also requisitioned in Great War, 1915–20), Trawler/Naval mine-sweeper, T: 231, mine 12/10/1940.

MTB no. 106 (1940), motor torpedo-boat, T: 18, foundered 16/10/1940.

HMS *Venetia* (1940), Destroyer, T: 1,300, foundered 19/10/1940.

MTB no. 16 (1939), motor torpedo-boat, T: 18, foundered 31/10/1940.

*Tilbury Ness* (1912), Trawler/Naval mine-sweeper, T: 1,300, bombed 01/11/1940.

SS *Letchworth* (1924), Collier from Blyth, T: 1,317, bombed 01/11/1940 (A. Firth et al, *London Gateway: Maritime Archaeology in the Thames Estuary*, pp. 59–61, 2012).

*East Oaze no. 60* (1888), Trinity House Light Vessel, T: 265, six lost, bombed 01/11/1940 (A. Firth et al, *London Gateway: Maritime Archaeology in the Thames Estuary*, pp. 69–70, 2012).

Engine from Luftwaffe aircraft, probably shot down 01/11/1940 (A. Firth et al, *London Gateway: Maritime Archaeology in the Thames Estuary*, pp. 61–2, 2012).

Trinity House. This organization was responsible for marking navigation channels with buoys (seen on the quayside here) and maintaining lightships and lighthouses. Two of her ships were sunk by enemy action in November 1940, just one year after this photo was taken at Trinity Buoy Wharf on the Thames. (© *Museum of London: PLA Collection 1101069*)

**SS *Herland*** (1924), Collier, T: 1,317, 3,500 tons of coal, eighteen lost, mine 07/11/1940.
***Reed*** (1911) (also requisitioned in Great War, 1914–19), Drifter/Naval mine-sweeper, T: 99, mine 07/11/1940.
***Muria*** (1914), Tug, T: 192, all crew lost, mine 08/11/1940.
**SS *Agamemnon*** (1914), T: 1,930, en route to Havana, bombed 08/11/1940.
**SS *Baltrader*** (1919), T: 1,699, en route from Seville, two lost, mine 08/11/1940.
***Argus*** (1909), Trinity House support vessel, T: 661, thirty-four lost, mine 11/11/1940.
    (A. Firth et al, *London Gateway: Maritime Archaeology in the Thames Estuary*, pp. 70–71, 2012).
***Restango*** (1913), Trawler, T: 1,699, struck Medway anti-sub boom 14/11/1940.
***Guardsman*** (1905) (also requisitioned in Great War, 1915–19), Tug/Navy tug, T: 1,699, two lost, mine 15/11/1940.

SS *Baltrader*. This ship, owned by the United Baltic Corporation, regularly carried food products to London. Seen here moored at Mark Brown's Wharf in 1937, she was sunk by a mine three years later. (© *Museum of London: PLA Collection 322780*)

SS *Batavier V*, moored in the Upper Pool in 1937. She made regular voyages between Rotterdam and London before being sunk by a torpedo in 1941.
(© *Museum of London: PLA Collection 320936*)

*Xmas Rose* (1918), Naval support vessel, T: 96, mine 11/11/1940.

*Amethyst* (1934), Trawler/Naval anti-U-boat patrol, mine ??/11/1940 (A. Firth et al, *London Gateway: Maritime Archaeology in the Thames Estuary*, pp. 64–65, 2012).

*Capricornus* (1917) (also requisitioned in Great War, 1917–19), Trawler/Naval minesweeper, T: 220, mine 07/12/1940.

SS *Actuality*, T: 311, cargo: cement en route to Norwich, six lost, mine 08/12/1940.

*Carry On* (1919), Trawler/barrage balloon vessel, T: 93, seven lost, mine 17/12/1940.

SS *Aqueity*, T: 370, 385 tons of cement en route to Sunderland, six lost, mine 17/12/1940.

SS *Beneficent* (1931), T: 2,944, coal en route from Sunderland, six lost, mine 17/12/1940.

SS *Inver* (1919), T: 1,543, coal en route from Blythe, seventeen lost, mine 17/12/1940.

SS *Belvedere* (1922), T: 869, cement en route to Tyne, four lost, mine 17/12/1940.

SS *Arinia* (1936), Tanker, T: 8,024, oil en route from Aruba, sixty lost, mine 17/12/1940.

*River Thames*, Tug, T: 88, mine 21/12/1940.

SS *Araby*, T: 4,936, 6,730 tons of cargo inc. wood from Santos, six lost, mine 27/12/1940.

# 1941

SS *Pinewood*, Collier, T: 2,466, en route to Blyth, six lost, mine 03/01/1941.

*New Spray* (1912) (also requisitioned in Great War, 1915–19), Trawler/barrage balloon vessel, T: 70, foundered in gale 03/01/1941.

*Lion*, Tug, T: 87 with barrage balloon vessel under tow, mine 06/01/1941.

SS *Strathearn* (1935), T: 683, en route to Harwich, sixteen lost, mine 08/01/1941.

*Desiree* (1912) (also requisitioned in Great War, 1914–19), Trawler/mine-sweeper, T: 213, mine 16/01/1941.

*Darogah* (1914) (also requisitioned in Great War 1914–19), Trawler/mine-sweeper, T: 221, mine 27/01/1941.

Navigational hazard: the Port of London Authority raises a sunken bombed wreck, an obstruction to other shipping. (© *Museum of London: PLA Collection 339291*)

*Boy Alan* (1914), Naval support vessel, T: 109, foundered 27/01/1941.

SS *Charlton* (1919), T: 1,562, cargo: 2,200t from Hartlepool, one lost, bombed 27/02/1941.

SS *Mexico* (1919), Tanker, T: 3,017, 3,823 tons oil from Curaçao, ten lost, mine 06/03/1941.

SS *Winkfield*, T: 5,679, 5,000 tons of cargo from Bombay, ten lost, mine 19/05/1941.

SS *Westavon*, T: 2,842, coal from Hartlepool, mine 30/05/1941.

*Ash* (1939), Trawler/Naval mine-sweeper, T: 530, mine 05/06/1941 (A. Firth et al, *London Gateway: Maritime Archaeology in the Thames Estuary*, pp. 67–68, 2012).

*Audacious*, Fishing vessel, T: 86, two lost, mine 15/06/1941.

*Devon County* (1910) (also requisitioned in Great War, 1915–19), Drifter/Naval mine-sweeper, T: 86, mine 01/07/1941.

*Receptive* (1913) (also requisitioned in Great War, 1915–19), Drifter/Aux Naval patrol, T: 86, mine 03/07/1941.

*Rosme*, Sailing barge en route to Ipswich with cargo of wheat, mine 03/07/1941.

*Lord St Vincent* (1929), Drifter/Barrage Balloon vessel, T: 115, mine 07/07/1941.

*MMS no. 39* (1941), Naval motor mine-sweeper, T: 226, mine 07/08/1941.

*Golden Grain*, Sailing barge, T: 101, three lost, mine 19/08/1941.

*Glen Alva*, Fishing boat, T: 6, two lost, mine 19/09/1941.

SS *Bradglen* (1930), T: 4,741, cargo of steel from Jacksonville, eight lost, mine 19/09/1941.

Sitting ducks: ships berthed in the port were easy targets for the Luftwaffe.
(*Mary Evans Picture Gallery:* © *London Fire Brigade 10794707*)

Fire down below: fire-fighters deal with a ship ablaze in the Surrey Docks.
(*Mary Evans Picture Gallery:* © *London Fire Brigade 10534569*)

Knocking off: reeling in the hoses, having contained an onboard fire at the Surrey Docks. (*Mary Evans Picture Gallery: © London Fire Brigade 10534568*)

**SS** *Vancouver*, Tanker, T: 5,729, 7,500t gasoline from Halifax, thirty-nine lost, mine 21/09/1941.

*Forerunner* (1911) (also requisitioned in Great War, 1915–19), Drifter/Naval mine-sweeper, T: 92, lost in collision 14/10/1941.

**SS** *Empire Ghyll* (1941), Collier, T: 2,011, from Sunderland, seven lost, mine 18/10/1941.

*Emilion* (1914) (also requisitioned in Great War, 1915–19), Trawler/Naval mine-sweeper, T: 201, mine 24/10/1941.

*Lucienne Jeanne* (1917) (Free-French crew working for Royal Navy), French trawler/Naval mine-sweeper, T: 286, mine 24/10/1941.

*Britisher*, Sailing barge, T: 95, two lost, sank 04/11/1941.

*Monarda* (1916) (also requisitioned in Great War, 1915–19), Drifter/Naval mine-sweeper, T: 109, mine 08/11/1941.

**MV** *Ryal*, Cargo: 350t steel en route to Middlesbrough, mine 21/11/1941 (A. Firth et al, *London Gateway: Maritime Archaeology in the Thames Estuary*, pp. 68–9, 2012).

## 1942

**SS** *Corfen*, Collier, T: 1,848, en route from Sunderland, one lost, mine 03/01/1942.

**SS** *Norwich Trader*, T: 217, en route to Norwich, seven lost, mine 03/01/1942.

**HMS** *Vimiera* (1917), Destroyer, T: 900, crew of ninety-one all lost, mine 09/01/1942.

**SS** *Quickstep*, T: 2,722, en route to Tyne, thirteen lost, mine 03/01/1942.

*HK Daniels*, Sailing barge, T: 65, wheat en route to Whitstable, mine 03/01/1942.
SS *Atlanticos*, T: 5,446, grain from St John's, one lost, mine 21/02/1942.
*Unique*, Sailing barge, T: 65, en route to Brightlingsea, two lost, mine 02/05/1942.
*Little Express*, Fishing smack, three lost, mine 04/05/1942.
*Maggie*, Fishing vessel, T: 6, all crew lost, foundered 17/06/1942.
SS *Linwood*, Collier, T: 992, 1,160t coal from Sunderland, three lost, mine 15/11/1942.
*Bankside*, Sailing barge, T: 77, flour from Burnham-on-Crouch, one lost, mine 19/12/1942.

## 1943–45

SS *Josefine Thorden* (1932), Tanker, 7,400t oil from Curaçao, fifteen lost, mine 06/04/1943.
SS *Dynamo*, T: 809, 400t en route to Hull, seven lost, mine 17/04/1943 (Firth, 2012, pp. 56–7).
SS *Moscha Kydoniefs* (1915), T: 3,874, grain from St John's, collision 09/05/1943.
*JBW*, Sailing barge, T: 72, two lost, mine 15/07/1943.
*Ocean Retriever* (1912) (also requisitioned in Great War, 1914–19), Drifter/Naval patrol vessel, T: 95, eleven lost, mine 22/09/1943.
SS *Norhauk*, T: 6,086, cargo inc. 1,000t military hardware, eleven lost, mine 21/12/1943.
SS *Newlands*, T: 1,556, from Liverpool, three lost, torpedo midget submarine 26/03/1945.

# Losses in the River Thames, September 1939 to May 1945

SS *Sheaf Crest*, T: 2,730, en route to Tyne, foundered 28/11/1939.
SS *Dalryan*, T: 4,558, en route to Ipswich, foundered 01/12/1939.
SS *Ursus* (1902), T: 1,499, cargo of vegetables to Rochester, foundered 15/12/1939.
SS *Amor*, T: 2,325, en route to Amsterdam, foundered 11/03/1940.
*Enchantress*, T: 56, Thames Sailing barge, air-raid on Victoria Docks 24/09/1940.
HMS *Cornwall* (1815, Bombay), 74-gun/training ship, bomb, Gravesend 24/09/1940.

HMS *Wellesley* was launched in 1815 as a seventy-two-gun naval warship. In later life she served as the training ship *Cornwall* but was badly damaged by bombing in September 1940. Although salvaged in 1948, she was then broken up; the oldest Royal Naval ship destroyed by the Luftwaffe in London. (*shipwreckology.com*)

*Lea*, T: 168, Tug, mine, Tilbury Basin 02/11/1940.

*Deanbrook*, T: 149, Tug, mine, Tilbury Basin 02/11/1940.

*Juno* (1937), paddle-steamer/AA defence, T: 642, bombed, Surrey Docks 19/03/1941.

**SS *Lunula***, Tanker, T: 6,363, cargo: 8,500 tons of spirits, mine, Shell Haven 09/04/1941.

*Coronation of Leeds*, Water tanker, mine, Shell Haven 22/04/1941.

*Gypsy*, Steam yacht/Aux Patrol Vessel, T: 261, bomb, Tower Pier 11/05/1941.

*Blue Mermaid*, Sailing vessel, T: 97, mine 09/07/1941.

*Little Express*, Fishing vessel, foundered, Kentish Flats 04/05/1942.

*Astevensa*, motor boat, bomb, Woolwich 21/10/1943.

*Naja*, Tug, T: 72, V-1 rocket, Upper Pool 12/07/1944.

**SS *Richard Montgomery*** (1943), T: 7,176, cargo: 6,862 tons munitions for Cherbourg, foundered Sheerness 15/08/1944.

**SS *Mount Othry*** (1919), T: 6,527, in collision with SS *Evinna* off Hole Haven 07/01/1945.

SS *Richard Montgomery*, carrying much-needed arms and ammunition, ran aground and sank with her lethal cargo in 1944 off Sheerness. (*Bobleroi.co.uk*)

Tower Bridge Tug *Naja*. Sunk by a V-1 rocket, July 1944, killing all six crew. Shown here laid up on foreshore after salvage. (© *London Metropolitan Archive Collage: Cross & Tibbs 35627*)

*Chapter Thirteen*

# Bombed in the London Blitz

In addition to the colliers, tankers, coasters and tugs that plied the working river, smaller wooden vessels also had a role to play in the complex activities of the port. These boats, propelled by oars or small engines, would be in demand for such tasks as transferring personnel from ship to shore. A selection can be seen in early twentieth-century views of the Pool of London.

The remains of half a dozen such small wooden vessels recorded by the Thames Discovery Programme team on the foreshore in central London almost certainly represent losses in the Blitz. Damaged by bomb blasts or shrapnel, loosed from their moorings and drifting on the tide, damaged

Boats and ships: even in the age of transatlantic steam shipping, the port still accommodated humble wooden working boats, as seen in the pre-war Pool of London. The remains of several similar vessels recorded by the Thames Discovery Programme were all in contexts suggesting loss in the 1940s' Blitz. (© *Museum of London: PLA Collection 11934*)

Off to war: a Thames skiff requisitioned for war work with the fire brigade, painted battleship grey. (*Mary Evans Picture Gallery:* © *London Fire Brigade 10534956*)

vessels ended up grounded on the muddy foreshore. This was a time of great shortages and so, if those boats had engines, these were removed and recycled, as were the more accessible upper planking and deck boards. However, the lower sections of the hull were simply left, often close to scatters of bomb debris, silting up in the thick mud of a foreshore that was rather less inviting than it appears today.

**Blackfriars no. 6** (site code ref. FCY a102) was recorded on the foreshore near Blackfriars Bridge, opposite what was once Bankside Power Station, now the Tate Modern. This boat may have been inundated and sunk following the ferocious bombing of the City warehouses on the adjacent waterfront on

Blackfriars no. 6: the Thames Archaeological Survey team washes remains of the vessel prior to recording. Note the entire port side had already been lost by 1998 (ref. FCY a012). (© *TDP*)

Blackfriars no. 6: extent of vessel remains exposed on the open foreshore in 1998. Ten years later, the rest of the boat had eroded out of the foreshore (ref. FCY a012). (© *TDP*)

the night of 10/11 May 1941. The remains represented part of the starboard side of a lightly-built, copper-riveted, clinker-planked vessel, some 7m in length from stem to stern. It was probably at least 1.2m in beam and presumably designed as a rowing boat, but with evidence that an engine had been added at a later date. This had been comprehensively subsequently stripped out after the vessel was abandoned.

**Custom House no. 2** (site code ref. FCY a106) was a small punt-ended lighter some 5.5m long and 1.8m in the beam, designed with rowlocks but its construction included plywood, perhaps evidence of a later repair. It had been

Custom House no. 2: the remains of a square-ended punt or lighter abandoned below a jetty next to Custom House Stairs and filled with silt (ref. TDP FCY a106). (© *TDP, N. Cohen*)

abandoned hard against the wooden posts of a jetty that had itself been replaced after the war with a concrete piled structure. One of those modern piles had been driven through the craft, oblivious to its presence, suggesting that by then it had been filled and covered in a thick blanket of silt.

Custom House no. 2: recording the vessel as part of a community archaeology training workshop (ref. TDP FCY a106). (© *TDP, N. Cohen*)

**Custom House no. 3** (site code ref. FCY a109) was a well-constructed clinker-built boat at least 8m in length and 3m in the beam. The presence of a number of repairs to her hull planking suggests a long and robust life. Initially sail and/or oar-powered, she had subsequently been modified to take a small engine. The lack of a bow suggests bomb or blast damage, perhaps the result of the V-1 rocket that destroyed the eastern range of the neighbouring Custom House and adjacent warehousing.

Custom House no. 3: partial exposure of sand and silt-filled vessel hull, with the stern in the foreground. The propeller (and presumably the engine) have been removed. The bow of the vessel is missing, perhaps broken off during an air-raid (ref. FCY a109). (© *TDP, N. Cohen*)

**Custom House no. 4** (site code ref. FCY a135) is only visible at extreme low tides, and thus has not been subject to full recording. Similar in form to FCY a109 (see above) but with more elegant lines, it has clearly been stripped virtually down to the keel of all reusable elements.

**Alderman's Stairs no. 1** (Foreshore Tower Hamlets (FTH)02 a121) lies close to Alderman's Stairs, just to the east of the City. The remains of this clinker-built wooden boat suggest that it was of similar dimensions to FCY a109 (see above). It is now much obscured by a spread of hastily-poured concrete, presumably marking an attempt to level up an uneven foreshore as London tried to get back to work after the Blitz.

## War and Peace: House Barges on the Thames and Medway

Apart from the human cost, the Luftwaffe's intensive bombing campaigns left London County Council with a severe housing crisis: the coloured maps

Custom House no. 4: this vessel is only exposed at exceptionally low tides. All the uppermost timberwork has been systematically stripped off, leaving just the bottom planking and some of the ribs (ref. FCY a135). (© *TDP, N. Cohen*)

Alderman's Stairs no. 1: outline of part of a wooden vessel, half covered with a spread of concrete (ref. TDP FTH a121). (© *TDP, N. Cohen*)

published in their surveys reveal the extent of the problem and the challenge it represented. The innovative solutions proposed and implemented included prefabs, new estates and even 'New Towns', but all this took time. One more informal solution was the marked increase in the number of houseboats that appeared on the Thames and on many other waterways. This made good use of obsolete barges and decommissioned naval craft now deemed surplus to

Alderman's Stairs no. 1: cleaning the inboard hull planking (ref. TDP FTH a121).
(© *TDP, N. Cohen*)

requirements in a (hopefully) more peaceful age. To the author's knowledge, there is no comprehensive account of the extent of this immediate post-war phenomenon, presumably precisely because of its unregulated informality. Nevertheless, examples of such practical repurposing have been recorded by the TDP team in Brentford and on other riverside sites.

# Chapter Fourteen

# The Thames, Operations DYNAMO and OVERLORD

## Dunkirk: Operation DYNAMO

In May 1940, the German army invaded France, and the Allied forces were all too rapidly overwhelmed. The British Expeditionary Force (BEF) found itself trapped on the exposed coast near Dunkirk, with the German army pressing in on them from the land and the Luftwaffe attacking them from the air. An emergency evacuation, code-named Operation DYNAMO, was hurriedly planned. Privately-owned ships, boats and barges from the coasts and rivers of southern England were requisitioned or volunteered for service to work alongside the larger vessels from the Royal Navy in the seemingly impossible task of rescuing the British army at the eleventh hour. The story of what followed is well-known, a tale of near tragedy turned on its head through the extraordinary courage of the crews that manned those 'Little Ships'.

### Thames Sailing Barges at Dunkirk

The Thames sailing barge (TSB) has a broad flat bottom, and is thus well suited to working off wide shallow beaches such as those at Dunkirk, where deep-draught shipping was unable to operate. The plan was that the armada of shallow-draft vessels, including the TSBs, would take the troops directly off the beach and ferry them to the larger ships anchored offshore. However, the entire operation had to be conducted under ferocious fire from the Luftwaffe, who made no distinction between soldiers or civilians, between Royal Navy vessels or fishing boats. Somehow, from 27 May to 4 June 1940, a staggering total of 338,266 soldiers were rescued, in twos and threes, in dozens or in hundreds, depending on the size of the vessels in that motley armada pulled together from London and the southern ports.

It is recorded that sixteen Thames sailing barges set out to do their bit in the summer of 1940. The exploits of the craft and their crews have been recorded in Frank Carr's *Sailing Barges*. Eight were lost on active service – a heavy price – and their names deserve to be remembered alongside those of mighty battleships. The lost barges were *Aidie*, *Barbara Jean*, *Duchess*, *Doris*, *Ethel Everard*, *Lady Roseberry*, *Lark Valonia* and *Royalty*.

Call to action: the 'Little Ships' set off down the Thames for Dunkirk.
(*Mary Evans Picture Gallery:* © *Ronald Grant Archive 1200781*)

Return journey: the 'Little Ships', crowded with troops evacuated from Dunkirk, make for home under fire. (*Mary Evans Picture Gallery:* © *Everett Collection 11000742*)

*Massey Shaw*: the local heroine returns from Dunkirk to her base at Blackfriars.
(*Mary Evans Picture Gallery:* © *London Fire Brigade 10535405*)

What of those that did make it home? David and Elizabeth Woods included the location of the seven Thames sailing barges that survived Dunkirk nearly fifty years later in their 1987 catalogue 'Last Berth of the Sailor Man', the term often used for those vessels. *Ena* was then at Ipswich, and was last recorded at Hoo in 2019, but its partner *H.A.C.* was broken up at Ramsgate. In 1987, *Beatrice Maud* was at Morwellham Quay and *Thyra* was at Poole, while *Glenway* was at Dolphin Yard, Colliers Creek before being sold

Abandoned ship: Thames Sailing Barge *Ena*, after a hard working life and valiant service at Dunkirk, lies forgotten in the mud at Hoo on the Medway in 2019. (© *Adam and Robert Kerry*)

in 2007 prior to a complete rebuild. *Tollesbury* was at Pin Mill in 1987; she sank in 2005, but was raised and is now under restoration at Standard Quay, Faversham. Finally, *Pudge* is still at Maldon, Hythe, restored and robustly active in 2018.

## Little Ships

However, it was not just Thames sailing barges that served at Dunkirk: famously, a range of 'Little Ships' took on the challenge of ferrying troops off the beach, including fishing boats, river launches, motor yachts, the fire-boat *Massey Shaw* and even the paddle-steamer *Medway Queen*. She was built in 1923 to take holidaymakers from Kent to the Thames Estuary resorts of Southend and Herne Bay. All that changed when she was requisitioned for war work in 1939 as a mine-sweeper and then, in 1940, played a significant role in the Dunkirk troop evacuations. In nine days, she made no fewer than seven journeys across the Channel, all under fire, saving some 7,000 troops. In addition, being armed with a 12-pounder, a Lewis gun and a crew of willing soldiers with Bren guns, she shot down three enemy aircraft for good measure. Seven of her crew received awards or were Mentioned in Dispatches for their exceptional endeavours. After the war, she returned to civilian life but was deemed unprofitable by 1985. After a long battle, she has now been restored through the hard work of the *Medway Queen* Preservation Society, and can be visited at her Gillingham berth.

Born survivor: Thames Sailing Barge *Pudge*, built a century ago, sailed to Dunkirk and back in 1940 but was still alive and well and working in Maldon in 2016. (© *CITiZAN*)

*Medway Queen*: converted from a pleasure boat to a naval mine-sweeper, HMS *Medway Queen* heads off to Dunkirk in 1940. (© *John Graves*, Medway Queen *Preservation Society*)

*Medway Queen*: Dunkirk 1940, viewed from the deck of the *Medway Queen*.
(© *John Graves*, Medway Queen *Preservation Society*)

*Medway Queen*: on her first voyage back to England from Dunkirk, although already fully loaded, the *Medway Queen* rushes to rescue the stricken *Brighton Belle*. All hands were brought home safely. (© *Eric Woodroffe*, Medway Queen *Preservation Society*)

By no means all of the vessels that served at Dunkirk returned safely: the *Abukir*, for example, packed with soldiers from the beaches, was sunk by a torpedo off the Kent coast with the loss of some 400 lives. Even for the vessels that did survive, the war was not yet over. Several of the civilian craft that had been requisitioned by the Admiralty for war work made the trip to Dunkirk and then returned to military duties. Two such vessels were the *Amethyst*, a trawler in peacetime, and the motor launch *Aisha*. Both were sunk by mines within six months of successfully saving lives in Operation DYNAMO.

## ML 286/River Launch *Eothen*
### (by Eliott Wragg with Suzanne Taylor)

The Thames Discovery Programme team has spent several seasons working in Isleworth recording one of the Dunkirk 'Little Ships', a river launch named *Eothen*, but she proved to have an even more illustrious history, seeing action in both world wars. Built just over a century ago, she started life as a naval motor launch, ML 286, a submarine-chaser. Even in the First World War (1914–18), shipping was targeted by German U-boats. One response from the Admiralty was to commission 550 fast, manoeuvrable motor launches, specifically designed to chase and sink enemy submarines. One such was ML 286, ordered from the Electric Launch Company of New York in 1915. Its first commander was the painter Geoffrey S. Allfree, initially commissioned as a sub-lieutenant in the Royal Naval Volunteer Reserve and who had served in the ill-fated Gallipoli campaign. In January 1918 he was made an official War Artist, but regrettably drowned when the vessel he was then commanding, ML 287, blew up just six weeks before the Armistice was signed.

As for ML 286, she survived the First World War, was decommissioned, sold off, then converted as a pleasure boat called *Cordon Rouge*. By 1940, she had been rechristened *Eothen* and was back on active service, taking part in the successful operations at Dunkirk to help ferry troops from the beaches to larger transport vessels. Although initially considered for more war work as a Thames patrol vessel, she was returned to civilian life.

She continued as a launch/houseboat for the next forty years until, in need of major repairs, she was brought into a boatyard at Isleworth in the 1980s. Unfortunately the costs of the necessary refit were more than the owners could afford, and she had to be abandoned. She was rediscovered there in 2015 by the Thames Discovery Programme team, following up a provisional identification made by Dr Antony Firth (Fjordr Ltd). Three annual survey sessions followed to record as much of the external elements of the (by now) badly degraded vessel as was possible in a constricted, muddy and overgrown tidal backwater.

It now seems that this particular vessel, ML 286, is the last known survivor of her class. However, it also seems that there are no surviving detailed plans of such craft. Thus the compilation of a more precise survey is of much increased importance, both as a record of these vessels and their important contributions to the allied victory in the First World War, but also her own particular heroics at Dunkirk in the second. A more detailed project plan was then developed, building on the initial surveys and the subsequent clearance of encroaching vegetation. Initial exercises in 3D laser scanning and photogrammetry have now been undertaken with some success, and the next phase,

*Eothen*/ML 286: stern view in 2017. The archaeological survey begins on the remains of this century-old warhorse. (© *TDP*)

for which detailed plans and funding applications have been prepared, could involve the complete excavation of this gallant and unique vessel. Such a scheme would bring together the experience and expertise of the National Museum of the Royal Navy, the Coastal Heritage Trust, MOLAS, Fjordr Ltd and the Thames Discovery Programme team. Meanwhile, background research on the vessel, her crew and her sister ships continues, thanks in particular to Suzanne Taylor and Sarah West.

## Thames Lightermen and Operation OVERLORD

### D-Day: The Allied Invasion Fleet in Normandy

At first light on the morning of 6 June 1944, the world's largest sea-borne invasion fleet appeared off the Normandy coast: the liberation of Nazi-occupied Europe had begun. There are many well-known images of the Allied troops and tanks storming onto the beaches code-named Utah, Omaha, Gold, Juno and Sword. What is less well-known is the vital role played by Thames lightermen in that truly historic event. The summary of their involvement is based on the testimony of the remarkable Edwin Hunt, who personally captained a fleet of 16 converted steel Thames swim-headed barges, crewed by 120 Thames lightermen, across the Channel to Gold Beach that day. The whole story has three phases: (1) Deception, 1942–44; (2) D-Day, 1944; and (3) Liberation, October 1944–45.

### Deception: A Second Front?

The deception began in 1942, when the Third Sea Lord, Admiral Sir Bruce Fraser, addressed a hastily-convened meeting in London of Thames lighter-men, who between them owned some 7,500 engineless barges or lighters, used for transshipping cargoes on the Thames and in its enclosed docks. He asked them if they could provide him with 1,200 of their best barges, at a time when London's river was working extra hard to ensure the safe and timely delivery of food and other essential supplies in the middle of a war. The Sea Lord's plan was to add engines and large hinged loading ramps to the bow of those Thames steel lighters – later called Power Barge Ramps (PBRs) – then berth them in a series of south coast ports. The aim was to fool German reconnaissance into thinking that a large fleet of military landing craft was being assembled for an imminent Allied invasion. Within three months, the lightermen had handed over the required barges, which were duly converted and assigned to various Channel ports. There then followed an extraordinary charade, in which this fleet of 'landing craft' was regularly moved from port to port under full naval escort. These manoeuvres successfully fooled the German high command into preparing for an attack on the north European coast. They consequently pulled German divisions back from Russia to reinforce the Channel ports, even though their Eastern Front was already buckling under pressure from the Red Army's advances. This bought time and space for our Soviet allies, who dramatically capitalized upon the opening of the fictitious 'Second Front', while Britain simultaneously began the long and detailed preparations for the real invasion.

## D-Day: Operation NEPTUNE

The War Office then decided that the decoy PBR barges were too good to waste and had them upgraded for genuine active service, which included fitting them out with 1,000hp Thorneycroft engines. This new fleet provided transport for motor vehicles, for fuel, for ammunition, for sundry supplies and was crewed by some 2,000 members of newly-raised Nos. Three and Four Group Royal Engineers, Inland Waterways Transport (IWT) section. The majority of these 'troops' were experienced Thames watermen and lightermen. After four months' training, the men, their barges and their vital cargoes joined forces with the navy and the army, and made the 100-mile crossing from the Solent to Normandy overnight on 5/6 June, in spite of the stormy weather. Working tirelessly until mid-October 1944, these powered barges ferried 440,000 tons of supplies to the beaches, as well as some 90,000 vehicles; as Edwin Hunt recalls, 'everything from tanks to toilet rolls'.

## Liberation: Starving Europe 1944–45

However, that was not the end of war service for the Thames lightermen. Having demonstrated their dedication and effectiveness under fire on the beaches of Normandy, they found themselves supplying the Allied armies by river and canal, as the troops bitterly fought their way town by town across France and the Low Countries. Those Thames crews were also there at the relief of Rotterdam, for example: a devastated city with no food, no electricity and no fuel, just a civilian population quite literally starving to death. The role played by London's lightermen and the IWT in the Second World War should never be overlooked or forgotten.

# Epilogue

## A Non-Combatants' War

It is right and proper that the nation consciously recognizes the role and the sacrifice played by the armed forces in the last war. Yet what of the non-combatants? For some, the Blitz is still a memory; for most, it is merely history, but continues to command attention. Its presence is still felt topographically and architecturally, in the ruined churches left as quiet reminders, and in the many monuments, memorials and plaques raised in remembrance. The merchant seamen's memorial at Tower Hill records the dreadful loss of life endured by those attempting to maintain London's crucial food and fuel supplies. The role of the fire service (who lost more than 700 fire-fighters across the nation in the conflict), the ARP and the other emergency services in the Blitz are rightly lauded and have their own memorials, either in print or in public monuments. That is as it should be: great courage and an unassuming heroism was shown by those uniformed and non-uniformed civilians. Yet the resolve of so many Londoners who, simply by 'keeping calm and carrying on' in those dark days and blacked-out nights, also needs to be recognized and remembered.

Counting the cost: funeral for fire-fighters who died during the Blitz.
(*Mary Evans Picture Gallery:* © *London Fire Brigade 10534631*)

IN MEMORY OF

JOAN BARTLETT, AGED 18
AND
VIOLET PENGELLY, AGED 19

MEMBERS OF THE AUXILIARY FIRE SERVICE

AMONGST THE FIRST SERVING FIREWOMEN TO DIE ON
DUTY DURING AN AIR RAID
ON
SEPTEMBER 18TH 1940

In remembrance: plaque in Millwall for Joan Bartlett and Violet Pengelly. (© *TDP*)

Front-line troops: the AFS in action. (*Mary Evans Picture Gallery: © London Fire Brigade 10793962*)

Women drivers: many women served in the emergency services and were prepared to work throughout the worst air-raids, as the ever-present helmets show.
(*Mary Evans Picture Gallery:* © *London Fire Brigade 10794321*)

Such prosaic heroics are too easily underestimated. The Thames-Flood teams, engineers and labourers alike, worked throughout the war profession-ally and effectively, but have no formal memorial. Next time you walk over Waterloo Bridge, remember its history: this magnificent bridge was built during the Blitz, initially opening in 1942. It was regarded as a national priority: Hitler's bombs were not going to get in the way. Also, if you read the inscription on the bridge, it records the name of the architect who designed it, and the LCC Chief Engineer who, in spite of everything, made it happen: Sir Thomas Peirson Frank. However, what wasn't recorded here is that the hard graft of his Thames-Flood Prevention Emergency Repairs team did

(*Above*) Aftermath: women and men worked together in the vital search-and-rescue work that inevitably followed every air-raid. (*Mary Evans Picture Gallery: © London Fire Brigade 10793650*)

(*Opposite, above*) 'Keep calm and carry on': the streets had to be kept free of bomb debris, a demanding but thankless task for the road gangs. (*LMA: © Cross & Tibbs Collection, 35614*)

(*Opposite, below*) Flood prevention: the not-so-young labourers employed by the Thames-Flood units worked during the air-raids to secure breached river walls, then spent many weeks building effective flood defences. (*TDP, P. Kennedy, TF66*)

(*Below*) Hungry and homeless: support was provided for these bombed-out children with no home to go to. (*© Mary Evans Picture Gallery: Grenville Collins Collection 10949678*)

Night shift: acrid smoke, shrapnel, falling debris and painfully long hours took their toll on these non-combatants, seen here in a make-shift first-aid post.
(*Mary Evans Picture Gallery:* © *London Fire Brigade 10534824*)

something else. They saved London from drowning – an even bigger story, and an even greater debt we owe to him and his team. So spare a thought for those secret heroes next time you enjoy a Waterloo sunset from that most elegant vantage point. Let those sundry patches of shuttered concrete still visible on various reaches of the river wall stand as their memorial.

\*   \*   \*

Since writing those words, it is heartening to record that a plaque has now been set up in Victoria Tower Gardens, a modest but welcome commemoration of the LCC's visionary Chief Engineer Sir Thomas Peirson Frank during

the Blitz and the work of his Thames-Flood team. This initiative was supported by the Institution of Civil Engineers, of which he served as a distinguished president. The unveiling ceremony in 2016 was attended by the extended Frank family, one, two and three generations on. Both that plaque and this book try to ensure that the debt owed by today's Londoners to that sorely tried-and-tested Blitz generation must not be forgotten. The resolute, proactive defiance of mere civilians did as much to change history as did the military machine.

# Bibliography

## Part One: The Blitz

Barker, T. and Robbins, M., *A History of London Transport*, Vol. II (1974).

Bates, L., *The Thames on Fire: The Battle of London River 1939–1945* (Terence Dalton, 1985).

Cantwell, J., *The Second World War: A Guide to Documents in the Public Record Office* (PRO Handbooks no. 15, HMSO, 1993).

Churchill, W., *The Second World War, Vol. II: Their Finest Hour* (Cassel, London, 1949).

Cooper, N., *London Underground at War* (Amberley Press, Stroud, 2013).

Dobinson, C., *AA Command: Britain's Anti-Aircraft Defences of the Second World War* (English Heritage, 2001).

Gardiner, J., *The Blitz: The British Under Attack* (HarperPress, London, 2010).

Graves, C., *London Transport at War 1939–45* (Almark Publishing, London, 1947).

Hill, M., *The London Blitz: September 1940–May 1941* (Chapmans, London, 1990).

HMSO, *Frontline 1940–1: The Official Story of the Civil Defence of Britain* (HMSO, London, 1942).

Hosteller, E., *The Island at War: Memories of War-Time Life on the Isle of Dogs* (London, n.d.).

Johnson, D., *The London Blitz: The City Ablaze, December 29th 1940* (London, 1980).

Kingwell, P., *Our Park. Friends of Southwark Park* (London, 2010).

Lobel, P. and Mills, J., *The Boroughs of Wandsworth & Battersea at War* (Sutton Publishing, 1990).

Lowry, B. (ed.), *20th Century Defences in Britain: Handbook of the Defence of Britain Project* (Council for British Archaeology, 1996).

Moshenka, G., *The Archaeology of the Second World War: Britain's Wartime Heritage* (Pen & Sword, Barnsley, 2013).

Neville, J., *The Blitz: London Then and Now* (Hodder & Stoughton, London, 1990).

Pope-Hennessey, J., *History Under Fire: 52 Photographs of Air Raid Damage to London's Buildings, 1940–41* (London, 1941).

Richards, J. and Summerson, J., *The Bombed Buildings of Britain: A Record of Architectural Casualties 1940–41* (London, 1942).

Richards, J. and Summerson J., *The Bombed Buildings of Britain: A Record of Architectural Casualties During the Whole Period of Air Bombardment 1940–1945* (London, 1947).

Saunders, A. (ed.), *London County Council Bomb Damage Maps 1939–45* (London Topographical Society, 2005).

Smith, V., *Defending London's River: The Story of the Thames Forts 1540–1945* (North Kent Books, Rochester, 1985).

Trout, E., 'Concrete Air Raid Shelters 1935–1941: A Study of the British Cement Industry's Influence on Public Policy', *Construction History: International Journal of the Construction History Society*, Vol. 32, No. 2 (pp. 83–107, 2017).

Walpole, N., *Hitler's Revenge Weapons* (Pen & Sword, Barnsley, 2018).

Ward, L., *The LCC's Bomb Damage Maps 1939–1945* (Thames & Hudson, London, 2015).

Whiting, C., *Britain Under Fire: Bombing Britain's Cities 1940–45* (Pen & Sword, Barnsley, 2014).

Woolven, R., 'Introduction' in A. Saunders (ed.), *LCC Bomb Damage Maps, 1939–1945* (London Topographical Society, No. 164, 2005).

Ziegler, P., *London at War 1939–1945* (Alfred A. Knopf, New York, 1995, second edition 2002).

## Part One: Thames Floods

Carlsson-Hyslop, A., 'Storm-surge Science: The London Connection 1928–1953', in J. Galloway (ed.), *Tides and Floods: New Research on London and the Tidal Thames from the Middle Ages to the 20th Century* (University of London, Centre for Metropolitan History Working Paper, series No. 4, pp. 45–56, London, 2010).

Galloway, J., 'Storm Flooding, Coastal Defence and Land Use around the Thames Estuary and Tidal River, *c.*1250–1450', *Journal of Medieval History 30* (pp. 1–18, 2009).

Galloway, J., 'Piteous and Grievous Sights: the Thames Marshes at the close of the Middle Ages' in J. Galloway (ed.), *Tides and Floods: New Research on London and the Tidal Thames from the Middle Ages to the 20th century* (University of London, Centre for Metropolitan History Working Paper, series No. 4, pp. 15–28, London, 2010).

Milne, A., *London's Drowning* (Littlehampton Books, 1982).

## Part One: London's Maritime History

Carr, R., (ed.), *Dockland: An Illustrated Survey of Life and Work in East London* (NELP/GLC, London, 1986).

Craig, C., *London's Changing Riverscape* (Frances Lincoln Ltd, London, 2009).

Ellmers, C. and Werner, A., *London's Lost Riverscape* (Viking, London, 1988).

Ellmers, C. and Werner, A., *London's Riverscape Lost and Found* (London: London's Found Riverscape Project, London, 2000).

Greeves, I., *London Docks 1800–1980: A Civil Engineering History* (Thomas Telford, London, 1980).

Pudney, J., *London's Docks* (London, Thames & Hudson, 1975).

Tucker, J., *Ferries on the Lower Thames* (Amberley Publishing, Stroud, 2010).

Watson, N., *A Century of Service 1909–2009: Port of London Authority* (London, PLA, 2009).

## Part Two: LCC's Rapid-Response Teams

Unpublished sources for LCC's Thames-Flood Prevention Emergency Repairs unit in the London Metropolitan Archive:

    LCC/CE/WAR/01/040 Thames-Flood Prevention papers
    LCC/CE/WAR/01/041 Depots
    LCC/CE/WAR/01/042 Depots & Second Line of Defence
    LCC/CE/WAR/01/043 Records & Plans
    LCC/CE/WAR/01/044 Borough Accounts
    LCC/CE/WAR/01/045 Particulars of Premises

### Obituary: Sir Thomas Peirson Frank, 1881–1951

https://mail.google.com/content/article/10.1680/iicep.1952.10946 (Source: ICE Proceedings https://mail.google.com/content/serial/iicep), Vol. 1, Issue 1, January 1952, pp. 113–114.

Milne, G., 'Rediscovering the Thames', in J. Galloway (ed.), *Tides and Floods: New Research on London and the Tidal Thames from the Middle Ages to the 20th Century* (University of London, Centre for Metropolitan History, Working Paper series, No. 4, pp. 57–62, 2010).

Milne, G., 'The Thames at War: A Secret History Uncovered', in N. Cohen and E. Wragg (eds), *A River's Tale*, pp. 100–111 (MOLA, London, 2017).

## Part Three: Emergency Services

Croad, S., *London's Bridges* (HMSO, London, 1983).

Hickin, W., *Fire Force: An Organisational History of the National Fire Service 1941–1948* (W.F.H. Publications, London, 2013).

Jackson, W., *London's Fire Brigades* (Longmans, London, 1966).

Wallington, N., *Great Fires of London: Images of the London Fire Brigade at Work since 1833* (Sutton Publishing, Stroud, 2001).

Part Four: Nautical Studies

Firth, A., Callan, N., Scott, G., Gane, T. and Arnott, S., *London Gateway: Maritime Archaeology in the Thames Estuary* (Wessex Archaeology Report No. 30, 2012).

Grehan, J., *Dunkirk: Nine Days that Saved an Army* (Pen & Sword, Barnsley, 2018).

Hewitt, N., *Coastal Convoys 1939–1945* (Pen & Sword, Barnsley, 2008).

Larn, R. and Larn, B., *Shipwreck Index for the British Isles*, Vol. 3 (Lloyds, London, 1996).

Milne, G., McKewan, C. and Goodburn, D., *Nautical Archaeology on the Foreshore: Hulk Recording on the Foreshore* (RCHME, Swindon, 1998).

Wragg, E., *Reports on Wreck Sites and Artifacts Recovered* (unpubl. for PLA, 2010).

Wragg, E., 'Boats and Barges: The Archaeology of Thames River Craft', in N. Cohen and E. Wragg (eds), *The River's Tale* (MOLA, pp. 87–99, 2017).

## Epilogue

Brooks, A., *London at War: Relics of the Home Front from the World Wars* (Pen & Sword, Barnsley, 2011).

# Index